Language BOOSTERS

Written by
Collene Dobelmann and Amy Stern

Editor: Maria Gallardo, MA
Senior Editor: Janet Sweet
Cover Illustrator: Rick Grayson
Designer/Production: Alicia Schulte
Art Director: Moonhee Pak
Project Director: Stacey Faulkner

Copyright © 2009 Creative Teaching Press Inc., Huntington Beach, CA 92649
Reproduction of activities in any manner for use in the classroom and not for commercial sale is permissible.
Reproduction of these materials for an entire school or for a school system is strictly prohibited.

Table of Contents

Introduction	3–5
How to Use This Book	6
Friends	7
Family	8
Pets	9
Hobbies	10
Sports	11
Staying Fit	12
Eating Healthy	13
Feelings	14
Careers	15
My Community	16
At the Movies	17
At the Mall	18
At the Bookstore	19
At a Restaurant	20
The Doctor's Office	21
The Dentist's Office	22
Holidays	23
On Vacation	24
On the Road	25
On the Water	26
In the Air	27
Nouns	28
Verbs	29
Adjectives	30
Adverbs	31
Sentences	32
Paragraphs	33
Synonyms and Antonyms	34
Prefixes and Suffixes	35
Idioms	36
Parts of a Book	37
Authors	38
Illustrators	39
Fiction	40
Nonfiction	41
Folktales	42
Biography and Autobiography	43
Write to Tell a Story	44
Write to Describe	45
Write a Friendly Letter	46
Write to Persuade	47
Context Clues	48
Summaries	49
Following Directions	50
Cause and Effect	51
Fact or Opinion	52
Telling Time	53
Money	54
Addition	55
Subtraction	56
Multiplication	57
Division	58
Greater, Less, or Equal	59
Estimation	60
Place Value	61
Fractions	62
Decimals	63
Temperature	64
Length	65
Capacity	66
Weight	67
Graphs	68
Geometry	69
Area	70
Perimeter	71
Plane Figures	72
Solid Figures	73
Angles	74
Problem-Solving Steps	75
Probability	76
Inverse Operations	77
Mammals	78
Fish	79
Birds	80
Insects	81
Spiders	82
Vertebrates	83
Invertebrates	84
Body Systems	85
Animal Defenses	86
Plant Adaptations	87
Ecosystems	88
Natural Resources	89
Conservation	90
Water Cycle	91
Electricity	92
Solar System	93
Geography	94
Native Americans	95
Explorers	96
National Landmarks	97
Our Government	98
Rules and Laws	99
Anne Hutchinson	100
Thomas Jefferson	101
Frederick Douglass	102
Clara Barton	103
Eleanor Roosevelt	104
Martin Luther King Jr.	105
Neil Armstrong	106
Answer Key	107–111
Language Proficiency Reference Chart	112

Introduction

Language Boosters provides 100 practice pages designed to support students' language proficiency through repeated exposure to fundamental components of language instruction, including vocabulary, word usage, comprehension, multiple-meaning words, and cognitive and written language. In addition, practice pages focus on common academic content themes to aid cross-curricular learning and align with language arts, math, science, and social studies curricula.

Research-Based Instruction and the Importance of Language Proficiency

As research has shown, word knowledge is the bridge to reading success and a key predictor of overall achievement in school. *Language Boosters* provides expert instruction in mastering the fundamentals of language proficiency to help all students develop the understanding and confidence necessary to learn the English language.

In addition, *Language Boosters* features word-building strategies that target intentional and systematic vocabulary instruction designed around meaningful everyday and academic topics. This research-based format is recognized as especially effective for English Language Learners who are not exposed to rich sources of word knowledge and indirect learning.

Support for English Language Learners

State standards require all students, regardless of language proficiency levels, to meet academic content standards. *Language Boosters* guides students toward meeting those challenging standards in the third-grade classroom and is geared for students who have reached an intermediate level of language proficiency.

While all students will benefit from repeated practice with the language skills and content themes presented, *Language Boosters* offers a variety of features to specifically support your English Language Learners. The 100 practice pages are presented in progressive order; align with language arts, math, science, and social studies curricula; and are based on the most current proficiency standards for English Language Development (see reference chart on page 112). Each practice page features repetition and predictability of skills and tasks through consistent wording of directions, repeating question formats, simple sentence structure, and numerous illustrations for strong visual reference.

Introduction **3**

Practice Pages

The five questions on each practice page follow the same consistent format:

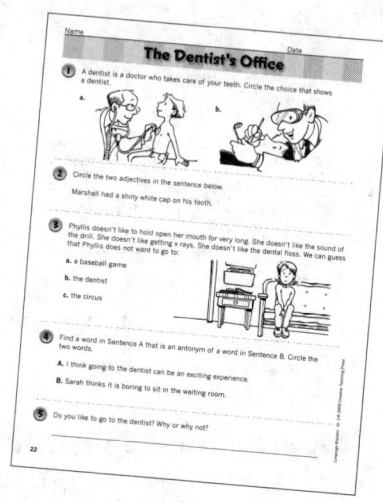

1. Vocabulary—everyday and academic words

2. Word Usage—grammar, syntax, mechanics, and other language conventions

3. Comprehension—context clues, word meaning, recall, and making inferences

4. Synonyms, Antonyms, and Multiple-Meaning Words—homographs and homophones

5. Cognitive and Written Language—responses to language, including personal connections

Vocabulary

These are specifically targeted words that students encounter in everyday (social) and curriculum-related (academic) settings. Academic vocabulary is more difficult to master because it is generally not specifically taught or used outside the classroom and draws on new vocabulary not typically encountered in everyday settings.

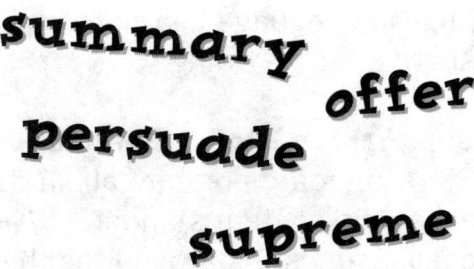

For additional learning support, *Language Boosters* provides a two-step scaffolding strategy to introduce academic vocabulary while building content knowledge. When introduced the first time, each academic vocabulary word appears in **boldface** with its definition. When presented the second time, the word usually appears with a definition prompt. When used subsequently, it appears without any additional support.

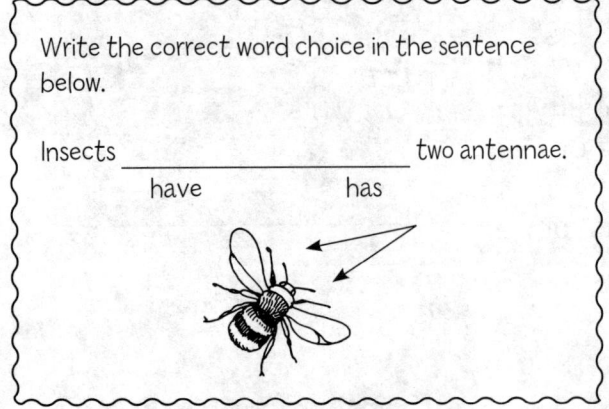

Word Usage

It is important for all students to understand and practice the often complex rules that govern the English language, such as sentence word order and necessary grammar and spelling rules. In addition to supporting questions in this category with helpful illustrations for visual reference, *Language Boosters* features short and simple sentences so as not to overwhelm the English Language Learner.

Introduction

Comprehension

Exposure to and use of words in numerous contexts promotes word learning and reading comprehension. To support the English Language Learner, *Language Boosters* features simple sentence structure and strong picture and language clues for questions in this category to help students gather meaning from words within context and to reinforce comprehension.

Jessica said, "Dad, when will you fix my bike? It needs to be repaired." What is wrong with Jessica's bike?

a. The bike is lost.

b. The bike is broken.

Synonyms, Antonyms, and Multiple-Meaning Words

It is important for all students to understand the need for using words that provide dimension, clarity, precision, and enrichment in the English language. This is particularly true for the English Language Learner, who may be relying on a limited amount of word knowledge to convey meanings or ideas. When describing a friend, for example, learning synonyms for the word *nice* enables students to describe more specific characteristics, such *kind*, *happy*, and *friendly*.

allowed

aloud

Cognitive and Written Language

A student's cognitive language typically exceeds his or her ability to produce oral or written language. This is especially true for English Language Learners, who may comprehend far more than the limited English that they are able to produce. It is important to provide students with multiple opportunities to interact with and respond to words and picture clues in a variety of ways to develop cognitive and written language proficiency. Consequently, the last question on each *Language Boosters* practice page features cognitive and written-language opportunities, such as identifying words with prefixes and suffixes, learning the meanings of idioms and other English language expressions, and responding to open-ended questions.

Dad came in with his umbrella. He said that it was raining cats and dogs out there. Circle the choice that shows what Dad meant.

a.

b.

How to Use This Book **5**

How to Use This Book

Use *Language Boosters* as a supplement to your English Language Arts or English Language Development curriculums to accentuate learning for both native English speakers and English Language Learners. Use the pages in order of appearance to make the most of the built-in scaffolding for the introduction of vocabulary, skills, and tasks. Or choose pages that fit with current themes or topics of study. Please note that students completing pages out of order may need additional instructional support. Present the practice pages using any of the instructional methods suggested below to aid in the development of listening, speaking, reading, and writing skills.

Individual Work
Depending on the ability levels of your students, have them complete pages individually for additional reinforcement with language skills or have them use pages together with guidance from a teacher or teaching assistant to work through the problems at a comfortable pace.

Paired Learning
Pairing students of differing ability levels or pairing a native English speaker with an English Language Learner can be an effective learning strategy. If working on a page such as Adjectives (page 30) or Mammals (page 78), students might take turns saying the names of objects on each page or finding antonyms. When one student gets stuck, his or her partner is there to lend support.

Small Group Activities
It has been found that language learners working in groups (cooperative learning) will achieve more, retain more in long-term memory, and use higher-level reasoning strategies more frequently when they learn information cooperatively.

Have students working in groups of five each take responsibility for one of the questions on each page, sharing answers with group mates, and consulting each other when stuck on a question. Small groups might also work clockwise in a circle, stating the names of objects presented on a page, or answering questions such as, "What is your favorite hobby?" (page 10) or "What are some other vertebrate animals?" (page 83).

Large Group Activities
Present large-group lessons using a transparency, document camera, or scanned practice page for use with your interactive white board to work through problems together with the class. Incorporate total physical response (TPR), a technique by which students demonstrate comprehension and answer questions through physical motions. Giving a "thumbs-up" or standing up might represent a yes answer, while "thumbs-down" or sitting down might represent a no answer. For example, when working on Natural Resources (page 89) you might call out items and say *Stand up if this is a renewable resource* or *Sit down if it is not a renewable resource*.

Friends

1. Mara and I laugh a lot. We are great friends. We enjoy being together. The word *enjoy* means:

a. to like something

b. to not like something

---

2. Circle the word in the sentence below that describes a feeling.

Friends make me feel happy.

---

3. I bumped into Michelle. She fell and hurt her knee. I felt bad. I gave her an apology. Circle the choice that shows an apology.

a.    b.

---

4. An **antonym** is a word that means the opposite of another word. Find a word in Sentence A that is an antonym of a word in Sentence B. Circle the two words.

A. My kitten's fur is soft.    **B.** The porcupine feels prickly.

---

5. Sometimes friends fight. Then they make up. They say, "I am sorry." What does it mean to make up?

a. to fight

b. to be friends again

7

Family

1 A parent is your mom or dad. Circle the choice that shows a boy with his parent.

a.    b.

2 An **adjective** is a word that describes a noun (a person, place, or thing). Circle the adjective in the sentence below.

Sasha has a tall brother.

3 Rico's grandmother lives with his family. She can't walk. She uses a wheelchair. Circle the choice that shows Rico's grandmother.

a.    b.

4 **Homophones** are words that sound the same. They are spelled differently and have different meanings. Find a word in Sentence A that is a homophone of a word in Sentence B. Circle the two words.

A. Louise is my aunt.      B. An ant bit my toe.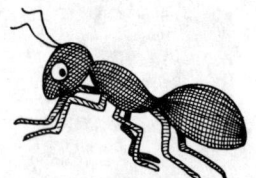

5 Write the names of the family members who live with you.

_____

Name _____ Date _____

Pets

1. Shelly's dog can sit, stay, and fetch a ball. Shelly's dog is a very good listener. Shelly trained her dog very well. The word *trained* means:

   a. taught

   b. yelled at

2. Rewrite the sentence below correctly. There are four mistakes.

   my pat turtle hid inside uv his shell

   _____

3. The sign in the shop window reads: *No pets allowed*. This means that:

   a. pets are welcome

   b. pets are not welcome

4. Find a word in Sentence A that is an antonym (means the opposite) of a word in Sentence B. Circle the two words.

   A. Some cats and dogs are friends.

   B. Other cats and dogs are enemies.

5. A **compound word** is a word that is formed by joining two smaller words. Combine the words below to write three compound words.

rattle + snake	butter + fly	black + bird
_____	_____	_____

9

Hobbies

1 Lena likes to collect dolls. She got two new dolls from her dad. Now Lena has 22 dolls. Circle the choice that shows the meaning of the word *collect*.

a.    b.

2 A **possessive noun** shows ownership by a person or thing. Adding an apostrophe and *s* (**'s**) makes most nouns possessive. Example: Roy**'s** baseball = the baseball that belongs to Roy. Rewrite the phrase below as a possessive noun.

bat that belongs to Tim   _____ bat

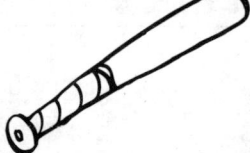

3 Trina's hobby is to bake. She likes to make muffins and cupcakes. She gives them to her friends. A hobby is something you do for:

a. fun   **b.** pay

4 Find a word in Sentence A that is an antonym of a word in Sentence B. Circle the two words.

A. Mario likes to play checkers.

B. He dislikes playing cards.

5 Complete the sentences below and draw a picture of your favorite hobby.

A hobby I enjoy is _____.

I enjoy this hobby because _____.

Name _____ Date _____

Sports

1 Swimming, soccer, and baseball are types of sports. Name three more sports.

_____   _____   _____

---

2 Circle the adjective (a word that describes a person, place, or thing) in the sentence below.

The fast swimmer won the race.

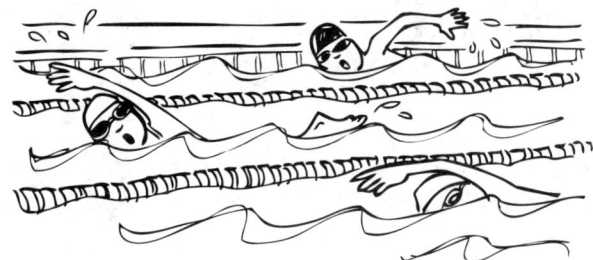

---

3 "Run, Joe, run! Bounce the ball down the court. Throw the ball in the hoop. Score two points for your team!" What sport is Joe playing?

a. football   **b.** basketball   **c.** soccer

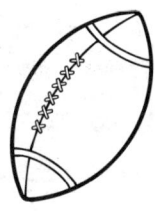      

---

4 A **synonym** is a word that has nearly the same meaning as another word. Find a word in Sentence A that is a synonym of a word in Sentence B. Circle the two words.

A. Can you run quicker than me?

B. Jenna swims faster than Todd.

---

5 A **suffix** is a group of letters added to the end of a word. The suffix -*est* means *most*. The suffix -*est* is added to words to compare more than two things. Circle the correct choice to complete this sentence.

Jimena is the _____ tennis player in the state.

a. strong   **b.** stronger   **c.** strongest

11

Name _____   Date _____

Staying Fit

1 Exercise makes your heart beat fast. It helps keep you healthy and strong. Circle the choice that shows a person doing exercise.

a.    b.

2 Write the correct word choice in the sentence below.

Liza _____ soccer to stay fit.
    play   plays

3 A snack is food we eat between meals. Healthy snacks give us vitamins and energy. They help keep us fit. Circle the choice that shows a healthy snack.

a.    b.

4 The sentences below contain homophones (words that sound the same but are spelled differently and have different meanings). Find a word in Sentence A that is a homophone of a word in Sentence B. Circle the two words.

A. We had to wait for the doctor to see us.

B. The nurse said my weight is healthy.

5 A **prefix** is a group of letters added to the beginning of a word. It changes the meaning of the word. Circle the word that has a prefix.

    a. fit   **b.** healthy   **c.** unhealthy

Name _____ Date _____

Eating Healthy

1 Alicia refused to eat her vegetables. She could not have dessert. The word *refused* means that Alicia:

    a. would not eat her vegetables   **b.** wanted to eat her vegetables

---

2 Write the correct word choice in the sentence below.

    Randy _____ beets and strawberries in his garden.
                grow   grows

---

3 Eating healthy food gives our bodies nutrients. Nutrients help our bodies grow and do work. Circle the choice that gives your body nutrients.

    a.    **b.**

---

4 Find a word in Sentence A that is a homophone of a word in Sentence B. Circle the two words.

    A. It's nice to meet new friends.    **B.** Some people do not eat meat.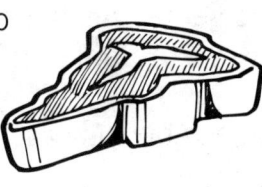

---

5 Complete the sentence below and draw a picture of your favorite healthy food.

    My favorite healthy food is

    _____.

Name _____   Date _____

Feelings

 The words *sad* and *mad* are feelings. Circle three more choices that describe feelings.

a. scared   **b.** upset   **c.** run   **d.** write   **e.** happy

 Some adjectives describe how people feel. Circle the adjective in the sentence below that describes how J.T. feels.

J.T. was lonely when her best friend moved away.

3. Today is Jackie's birthday. She is having a party. Jackie feels excited. Circle the choice that shows how Jackie feels.

a.    b.

4. The sentences below contain synonyms (words that have nearly the same meaning). Find a word in Sentence A that is a synonym of a word in Sentence B. Circle the two words.

A. Angela was mad because her brother pushed her.

B. Her brother was angry because Angela teased him.

 Answer the question below and draw a picture that shows how you are feeling.

How are you feeling today?

_____

Name _____   Date _____

Careers

1. My mom is a schoolteacher.
She loves her career.
Teaching is important to her.
A career is:

   a. a job   **b.** an office

2. Circle the adjective in the sentence below.

Rena is an architect who designs tall buildings.

3. Tomas loves animals. He likes to help sick or hurt animals. He wants to be a veterinarian when he grows up. Circle the choice that shows the veterinarian.

a.    **b.**

4. Find a word in Sentence A that is a synonym of a word in Sentence B. Circle the two words.

A. The librarian is a quiet person.

B. She likes a hushed workplace.

5. A suffix is a group of letters added to the end of a word. Add the suffix *-ful* to the word *success* to complete the sentence.

Ronnie's mother is a success_____ volleyball coach.
Her team wins many games.

15

Name   Date

My Community

1 A community is a group of people who live and work in the same place. Circle the choice that shows a person in your community.

a.    b.

2 Write the correct word choice in the sentence below.

A mail carrier _____ a person who works
                          is   are

in your neighborhood.

3 A firefighter works hard to put out fires. A doctor works hard to keep us healthy. A teacher works hard to:

a. help us learn

b. help us swim

4 Find a word in Sentence A that is a homophone of a word in Sentence B. Circle the two words.

A. The mail carrier delivered eight letters today.

B. I ate a huge chocolate chip cookie!

5 A firefighter works in your community. Name three more people who work in your community.

_____   _____   _____

Name _____   Date _____

At the Movies

 Sharon loves watching movies. Her favorite movies are about animals. Circle the choice that shows a movie.

a.    b.

 Circle the word in the sentence below that tells *how* Angela watched the movie.

Angela quietly watched the movie.

 Wendy's family went to the movies. They all got snacks before the movie started. When did they get snacks?

a. They got snacks first.

b. They got snacks when the movie was over.

 Draw a line from each sentence to the correct picture.

1. Be quiet and watch the movie!   a.

2. My watch doesn't tell the correct time.   b.

 Movies can be funny, sad, or even scary. What kinds of movies do you like to watch? Complete the sentence below.

I like to watch _____ movies because_____.

17

Name Date

At the Mall

1 There are many different kinds of stores at the mall. Most stores there offer clothing. *Offer* means:

a. to buy

b. to sell

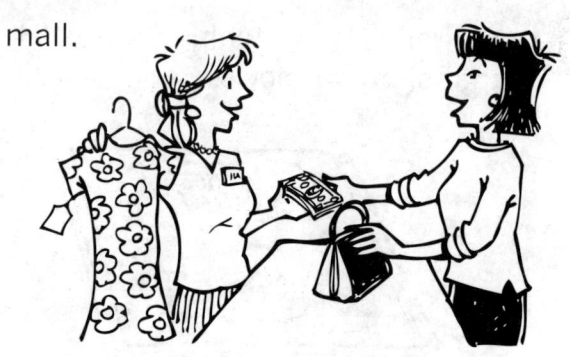

2 A **verb** is a word that tells what someone or something is doing. Circle the verb in the sentence below.

We purchased a puppy at Bill's Pet Shop.

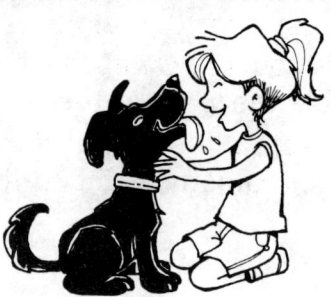

3 Sally tried on three dresses. The first one was too small. The second one was too big. The third one was just right, but Sally found a hole in the dress. Where is Sally?

a. in a shoe store **b.** in a clothing store

4 Circle the correct meaning of the word *shop* in the sentence below.

I shop at the mall every weekend.

a. to buy things in stores **b.** a place where things are sold

5 Combine the words below to make four compound words (words that are formed by joining two smaller words).

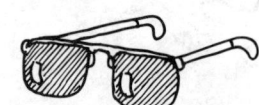

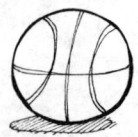

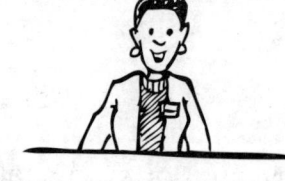

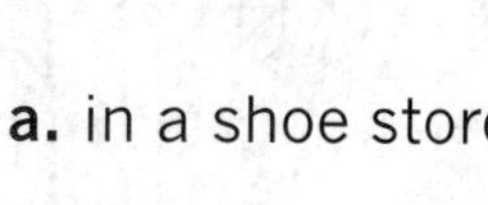

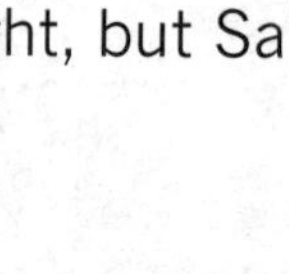

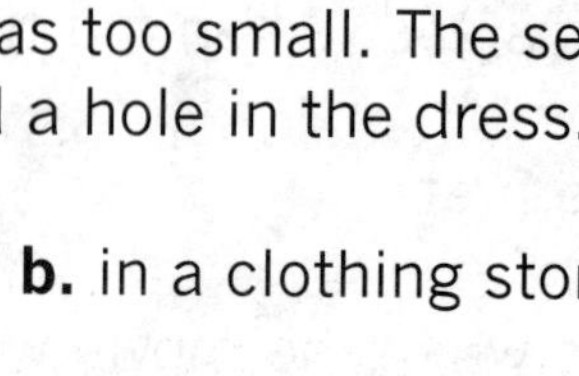

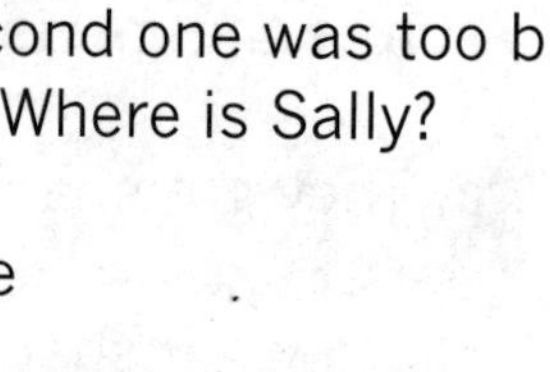

sun ball sales glasses super clerk basket market

______ ______ ______ ______

Name _____   Date _____

At the Bookstore

 You can buy books at a bookstore. Circle the choice that shows a bookstore.

a.  b.

 English has four sentence types that use different ending punctuation. A **statement** tells you something and ends with a period. A **question** asks you something and ends with a question mark. An **exclamation** shows strong feeling or surprise and ends with an exclamation point. A **command** tells you to do something and can end with either a period or an exclamation point. Identify the sentence type below.

Where will Enrique buy books?

a. statement   **b.** question   **c.** command   **d.** exclamation

 Daniel likes to read. He bought a book about dogs and a magazine about hiking. He also bought a newspaper to use for a school project. Where is Daniel?

a. in a store   **b.** in a bookstore

 Find a word in Sentence A that is a homophone of a word in Sentence B. Circle the two words.

A. Molly read her story aloud.

B. I am not allowed to talk while she reads.

 What books do you look for at a bookstore?

_____

Name _____   Date _____

At a Restaurant

1. Henry loves to go out to eat. He eats in a restaurant. Circle the choice that shows Henry eating in a restaurant.

a.    b.

2. A **noun** is the name of a person, place, or thing. Circle the three nouns in the sentence below.

Emmanuel had fun in the restaurant.

3. Draw a line from each sentence to the correct picture.

1. My mom is reading the menu at a restaurant.   a.

2. My mom is reading a recipe in a book.   b.

4. Find a word in Sentence A that is a homophone of a word in Sentence B. Circle the two words.

A. The flowers on the table are real, not fake.

B. Vidal goes fishing with his rod and reel.

5. What is the name of your favorite restaurant?

Name _____   Date _____

The Doctor's Office

 I love going to the doctor. I never cry, even if I get a shot! The doctor gives me stickers. Circle the choice that shows a doctor.

a.    b.

---

2 Rewrite the sentence below correctly. There are five mistakes.

dr turner gived me medicine for my cough

_____

---

3 Julio had the stomach flu. He drove to the doctor for a check-up. Circle the choice that shows the type of doctor he went to see.

a.    b.

---

4 Draw a line from each sentence to the correct picture.

1. She sat on her mom's lap in the doctor's office.   a.

2. Yesenia ran one lap around the track.   b.

 When do you go to the doctor?

_____

21

Name   Date

The Dentist's Office

1 A dentist is a doctor who takes care of your teeth. Circle the choice that shows a dentist.

a. 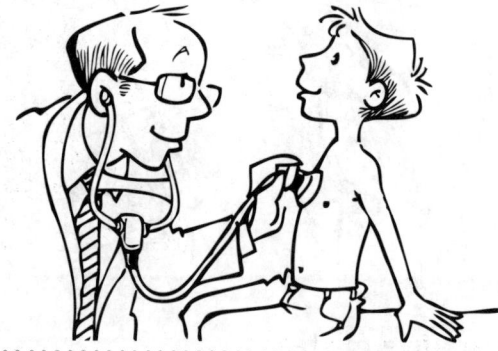   b.

2 Circle the two adjectives in the sentence below.

Marshall had a shiny white cap on his tooth.

3 Phyllis doesn't like to hold open her mouth for very long. She doesn't like the sound of the drill. She doesn't like getting x-rays. She doesn't like the dental floss. We can guess that Phyllis does not want to go to:

a. a baseball game

b. the dentist

c. the circus

4 Find a word in Sentence A that is an antonym of a word in Sentence B. Circle the two words.

A. I think going to the dentist can be an exciting experience.

B. Sarah thinks it is boring to sit in the waiting room.

5 Do you like to go to the dentist? Why or why not?

_____

22

Name _____ Date _____

Holidays

1 A holiday is a special day. School is closed for many holidays. Circle the choice that is a holiday.

   a. Presidents' Day   **b.** Friday

2 Rewrite the sentence below correctly. There are five mistakes.

we celebrate valentine's day in february

_____

3 The Fourth of July is an important U.S. holiday. Fireworks sparkle and pop high in the sky! Circle the choice that shows fireworks.

   a.   **b.**

 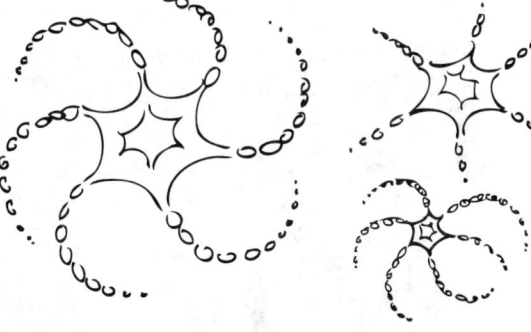

4 Find a word in Sentence A that is an antonym of a word in Sentence B. Circle the two words.

   A. It was a normal day at school.

   B. A holiday is a special day.

5 What is your favorite holiday?

_____

23

Name							Date

On Vacation

 Giovanni's family took a vacation. They went far away. They had fun on their trip. Circle the choice that shows a vacation.

a.					b.

 An **adverb** is a word that describes a verb. It often tells how, when, or where something happens. Circle the adverb in the sentence below.

Lupita swam quickly in the pool.

 Tara went on vacation. She went to the beach. She swam in the ocean. Circle the choice that shows Tara at the beach.

a.					b.

 "Have a nice trip," said Mrs. Burton. "I'll see you when you return." In this sentence, the word *trip* likely means:

a. a vacation					b. to fall down

 Does your family go on vacation? Where?

_____

24

Name _____ Date _____

On the Road

1 An automobile is a car. Circle the choice that shows an automobile.

a.  b.

---

2 Circle the two nouns (words that name a person, place, or thing) in the sentence below.

The tires need air.

---

3 Drivers must obey traffic laws to stay safe. We must stop at red lights and stop signs. We must wear our seat belts. What does it mean to obey?

a. to follow rules    **b.** to not follow rules

---

4 Find a word in Sentence A that is a synonym of a word in Sentence B. Circle the two words.

A. It is unsafe to drive too fast.

B. Lolly got a ticket for being a speedy driver.

---

5 An **idiom** is a phrase that means something different than what it says. We were ready to get in the car. Mom said, "Let's hit the road!" Circle the choice that shows what Mom meant.

   b.

25

Name _____   Date _____

On the Water

 A barge is a long, flat-bottomed boat. It carries heavy loads. Circle the choice that shows a barge.

a.   b.

 Ruby likes sailing. She has all the equipment she needs. Add an apostrophe and *s* (**'s**) to show that each item belongs to Ruby. Example: Ruby's sailboat

      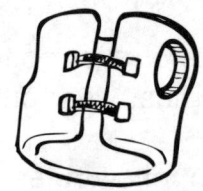

a. _____ anchor   b. _____ deck   c. _____ life jacket

 A boat sails on the water. It can sail in a river, lake, or ocean. Many people enjoy riding on boats. Circle the choice that shows a boat.

a.   b.

 Find a word in Sentence A that is an antonym of a word in Sentence B. Circle the two words.

A. A raft can float on the water.   **B.** A rock sinks under the water.

5. The Bend family had been on their boat for eight hours. They were tired and wanted to go home. They were ready to call it a day. The idiom *call it a day* is a phrase that means:

a. to stop what you are doing   b. to call mom on the telephone

Name _____   Date _____

In the Air

 An airplane has powerful engines that help it fly. Circle the choice that shows an airplane.

a.    b.

 Circle the verb (the word that tells what something does) in the sentence below.

The helicopter hovered in the air.

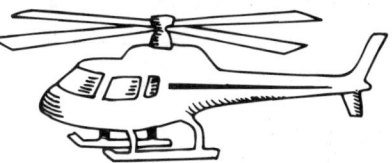

 A rocket flies straight up into the sky. Rockets go into outer space. Most rockets that go into outer space cannot be reused. This means that these rockets:

a. can be used only one time   b. can go into space many times

 Find a word in Sentence A that is a homophone of a word in Sentence B. Circle the two words.

A. We rode in a plane to visit Papa.

B. Papa's house is on a flat plain in Kansas.

 Dad came in with his umbrella. He said that it was raining cats and dogs out there. Circle the choice that shows what Dad meant.

a.    b.

27

Name _____ Date _____

Nouns

 Circle the three words below that are nouns.

a. ball   **b.** tall   **c.** dog   **d.** boy   **e.** sad

 Circle the two nouns in the sentence below.

The cup is full of juice.

 A **proper noun** names a certain person, place, or thing. Every proper noun begins with a capital letter. Circle the proper nouns below.

a. Sally Ride   **c.** astronaut

b. American   **d.** woman

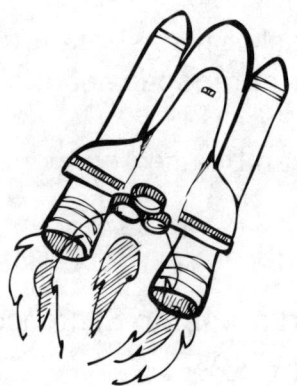

4 Find a word in Sentence A that is a homophone of a word in Sentence B. Circle the two words.

A. I have black hair.   **B.** A hare hopped across the road.

 Look around your classroom. Write the words for three nouns that you see.

_____   _____   _____

Name Date

Verbs

1 Circle the two words below that are verbs (words that tell what someone or something is doing).

    a. throw   **c.** game

    b. catch   **d.** baseball

2 Identify this type of sentence: Now I understand what a verb is!

    a. statement   **b.** question   **c.** command   **d.** exclamation

3 Allister rides his bike every morning. Then he jogs. After that, he swims. Circle the choice that shows what Allister likes to do.

a.    **b.**

4 Circle the verbs that are antonyms.

    a. Renee smiles when she is happy.   **b.** Ted frowns when he is mad.

5 Write three verbs below that tell what you do on the playground.

_____ _____ _____

29

Name _____ Date _____

Adjectives

1 Adjectives include number words and color words. Circle the adjective in each phrase below.

a. pretty swanb. twoc. blue dress

2 Rewrite the sentence below correctly. There are three mistakes.

the happy boy pet the littel puppy

_____

3 Read the story. Circle the three adjectives.

The bright sun shone on the flower. The little flower grew and grew. Soon the flower was very large.

4 Circle the adjectives that are synonyms.

a. The cold shower felt good.b. I swam in the cool water.

5 Write three adjectives below that describe your classroom.

_____

30

Name _____   Date _____

Adverbs

1 Circle the adverb (a word that tells how, when, or where something happens) in each sentence below.

    a. Alex ran quickly.   **b.** The dog barked loudly.   **c.** The baby cried sadly.

2 Rewrite the sentence below correctly. There are three mistakes.

    the shoemaker workt busily

    _____

3 Jack is taking a math test. He must add and subtract. He must answer each question very:

    a. easily

    b. nicely

    c. carefully

4 Find a word in Sentence A that is an antonym of a word in Sentence B. Circle the two words.

    A. Jennifer walked slowly.   **B.** Karen ate quickly.

5 Write an adverb for each sentence below that tells how you do each action.

    I do my homework _____.

    I run _____ around the track.

    I speak _____ in the library.

Name _____ Date _____

Sentences

 A **complete sentence** tells what someone or something does or says. Circle the choice below that is a complete sentence.

   a. Asher loves to draw.

   b. Loves to draw.

 Identify this type of sentence: Put your book in your desk.

   a. statement   **b.** question   **c.** command   **d.** exclamation

 Julie loves to write stories. She always uses complete sentences. Circle the choice that shows what Julie likes to do.

   a.    **b.**

 Write the correct word in the sentence below.

   We _____ the question with ease.
         red   read

 Ask a person who sits near you a question. Write it below.

   _____

Name _____ Date _____

Paragraphs

1 A **paragraph** is a group of sentences. The sentences in a paragraph focus on the same thought or idea. This means that a paragraph:

  a. describes one main topic   **b.** describes many different topics

2 Circle the two nouns in the sentence below.

Your story must have two paragraphs.

3 You must indent the first line of a paragraph. When you indent, you leave a small space before beginning the paragraph. Circle the choice that shows an indented paragraph.

a. 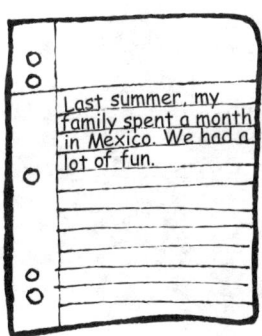   b.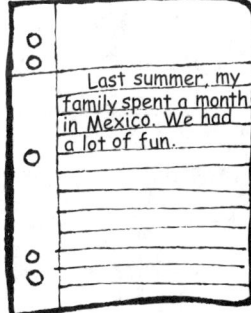

4 Write the correct word choice in the sentence below.

My paragraph has _____ sentences.
                         for   four

5 Draw a line to match each compound word to its correct picture.

schoolhouse   bookcase   bookmark   textbook

a.    b.    c.    d.

33

Name Date

Synonyms and Antonyms

 Circle the two pairs of words that contain antonyms.

    a. up–down   **b.** happy–glad   **c.** win–lose   **d.** heavy–wrong

 Identify the type of sentence below.

Tyler opened and shut the window.

    a. statement   **c.** command

    b. question   **d.** exclamation

 Jessica said, "Dad, when will you fix my bike? It needs to be repaired." What is wrong with Jessica's bike?

    a. The bike is lost.

    b. The bike is broken.

4 Find a word in Sentence A that is a synonym of a word in Sentence B. Circle the two words.

    A. Jeanne likes to go to the zoo.   **B.** Michelle enjoys chopping wood.

 Write a synonym for *sad* on the line below.

_____

34

Name _____   Date _____

Prefixes and Suffixes

 Circle the word below that has a prefix (a group of letters added to the beginning of a word).

I wrap the present. My brother unwraps the present.

 Rewrite the sentence below correctly. There are four mistakes.

ms thomas told us to reread the paragraph

_____

 Mira's puppy is playful. He likes to catch balls. He likes to chase cats. *Playful* has a suffix. What does the word *playful* mean?

a. full of play

b. tired

 Find a word in Sentence A that is an antonym of a word in Sentence B. Circle the words.

A. A prefix is added to the beginning of a word.

B. A suffix is added to the end of a word.

 Write a word below that has a prefix. Then write a word below that has a suffix.

Prefix _____   Suffix _____

Name _____ Date _____

Idioms

1 Learning the meanings of different idioms can be confusing. For example: *An apple a day keeps the doctor away* means eating good food will keep you healthy. Which phrase below is probably an idiom?

a. live it up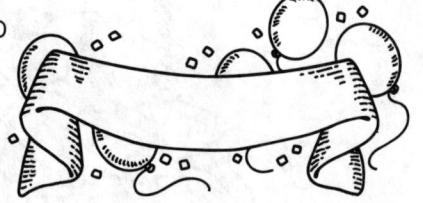

b. go to school

2 Rewrite the sentence below correctly. There are three mistakes.

idioms can be difficult to lern

_____

3 The idiom *break a leg* means to wish someone good luck. The idiom *shake a leg* means to hurry up. Which idiom would you say to a friend who is starring in the school play?

a. shake a leg

b. break a leg

4 Find a word in Sentence A that is a homophone of a word in Sentence B. Circle the two words.

A. "Feeling blue" is an idiom. It means feeling sad.

B. Patricia blew out the candles.

5 Something that is described as *A-OK* is absolutely fine. Circle the choice that shows something that is A-OK.

a.

b.

Name _____ Date _____

Parts of a Book

1 The **title page** is at the beginning of a book. It shows the title of the book and the names of the author and the illustrator. Circle the choice that shows a title page.

a.

b.

2 Write the correct word choice in the sentence below.

That is a thick book. It has lots of _____.
                                          page   pages

3 Carlotta read the first chapter of *Charlotte's Web*. It made her want to read the second chapter. Circle the choice that is probably true.

a. Carlotta does not like the book.

b. Carlotta likes the book.

4 Find a word in Sentence A that is a synonym of a word in Sentence B. Circle the two words.

A. I read the second chapter of the book.

B. I liked that part of the book.

5 Tony is the shortest boy in his class. Everyone was surprised to see what a good basketball player he is. The teacher said, "Don't judge a book by its cover!" The teacher means that you shouldn't judge people by:

a. the books they read

b. how they look

Name   Date

Authors

1 An **author** is a person who writes books. Circle the choice that tells the author's name.

   a. My Pet Pelican

   b. Alan Hentz

2 Identify this type of sentence: Do you like to write stories?

   a. statement   b. question   c. command   d. exclamation

3 An author writes a story based on an idea. Circle the choice below that shows a student who has an idea.

   a.   b.

4 Find a word in Sentence A that is a homophone of a word in Sentence B. Circle the two words.

   A. I write stories.   B. I use my right hand.

5 Who is your favorite author?

   _____

38

Name _____   Date _____

Illustrators

1 An **illustrator** is the person who draws art for a book. What did the illustrator draw for this book cover?

_____

2 Anna draws dogs and cats.

Is the word *draws* a noun or a verb?

_____

3 Write the correct word choice in the sentence below.

Everyone likes Jeremiah's artwork. He wants to _____ books one day.
                                                       illustrate   write

4 Draw a line from each sentence to the correct picture.

1. I like to paint pictures.   a.

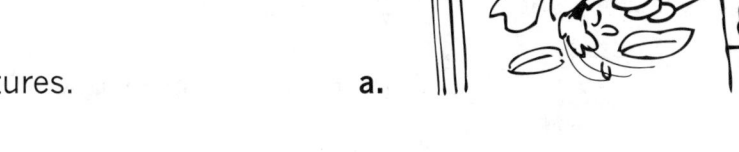

2. I spilled the black paint.   b.

5 Are you a good illustrator? Why or why not?

_____

Name _____   Date _____

Fiction

1) **Fiction** is a make-believe story that is not real. Circle the choice below that is fiction.

   a. *The Biography of Abraham Lincoln*   b. *Alice in Wonderland*

---

2) Identify this type of sentence: I love that book!

   a. statement   c. question

   b. command   d. exclamation

---

3) Jeffrey likes to read quietly. Jay likes to read out loud. Circle the choice that shows Jeffrey.

   a.   b.

---

4) Write the correct word choice in the sentence below.

   "Please _____ your story to the class," said Mrs. North.
             reed   read

---

5) Write the name of your favorite fiction book.

_____

40

Name _____   Date _____

Nonfiction

1 **Nonfiction** is a story about real people and true events. Circle the choice below that is nonfiction.

  a. *The Biography of Abraham Lincoln*   **b.** *Alice in Wonderland*

2 Circle the verb in the sentence below.

  Alexandria enjoys books about horses.

3 Many nonfiction books have a **glossary.** A glossary is a mini dictionary in the back of a nonfiction book. A glossary is used to:

  a. find the pages in a book   **b.** find the meanings of words

4 Write the correct word choice in the sentence below.

  Silvia loves to _____ nonfiction stories.
                    write   right

5 Write the name of your favorite nonfiction book.

  _____

41

Name _____   Date _____

Folktales

1 **Folktales** are very old stories that have been told for many years. Folktales are fiction. Circle the choice below that is a folktale.

a. The Wonderful World of Ants

b. Stone Soup by Marcia Brown

2 To form the **plural for most words that end in -y,** you must change the -y to -i and then add -es to the end of the word. For example: fl**y**–fl**ies**; cherr**y**–cherr**ies.** Write the plural form for each of the following nouns:

a. folktale _____   c. biography _____

b. story _____   d. author _____

3 Simone acted in a play. The play was called "The Drinking Gourd." The play was a folktale. It was make-believe. This play was:

a. fiction

b. biography

c. nonfiction

4 Circle the homophones in the sentence below.

Miguel is allowed to read the folktale aloud.

5 Write the name of your favorite folktale.

_____

Name _____ Date _____

Biography and Autobiography

1. A **biography** tells about a person's life. Circle the choice below that is a biography.

a. All About Cats

b. Abraham Lincoln

2. Identify the type of sentence below.

There are many biographies about Harriet Tubman.

a. statement c. question

b. command d. exclamation

3. If an author writes a book about another person's life, it is a biography. If an author writes a book about his or her own life, it is an **autobiography.** Frida Kahlo was a famous Mexican artist. The author Hayden Herrera wrote a book about Frida Kahlo's life. This book is:

a. a biography

b. an autobiography

4. Find a word in Sentence A that is a synonym of a word in Sentence B. Circle the two words.

A. A biography is usually about a famous person.

B. A biography is usually about a well-known person.

5. A biography is a story about _____

_____

43

Name _____ Date _____

Write to Tell a Story

1 We write for different reasons. One reason to write is to tell a story. Circle the choice below that tells a story.

a. [illustration of boy washing car with "Car Wash $5" sign]

b. [illustration of book "THE VERY HUNGRY CATERPILLAR by Eric Carle"]

2 Circle the two verbs in the sentence below.

Amber loves to write stories.

3 When Carlos was five years old, his family left Mexico to go live in California. They packed all of their things and drove all the way there. It was so exciting for them to arrive at their new home! How did Carlos's family get to California?

a. on a plane   **b.** on a ship   **c.** in a car

4 Find a word in Sentence A that is a homophone of a word in Sentence B. Underline the two words.

A. Rapunzel had beautiful long hair.

B. My favorite story is "The Tortoise and the Hare."

5 What is your favorite story?

_____

Name _____   Date _____

Write to Describe

1. We write for different reasons. One reason to write is to describe. When you describe something, you help the reader picture it. This means you:

   a. draw a picture with colorful paints

   b. use specific words to tell about something

2. Circle the noun in the sentence below.

   Please describe how to make a sandwich.

3. Peter loves chocolate chip cookies. Peter wrote the recipe for making the cookies. He wrote how the cookies will look and taste. Peter wrote a:

   a. description

   b. story

4. Anna likes to write long stories. Circle the antonym of the word *long*.

   a. wild   **b.** short   **c.** pretty

5. Describe your favorite pair of shoes. Tell their size, color, and special purpose.

_____

_____

_____

_____

45

Name _____   Date _____

Write a Friendly Letter

1 A letter to a friend begins with a **greeting**. Circle two choices below that are greetings.

   a. Dear Martin,   **b.** Sincerely,   **c.** Hello!   **d.** Yours truly,

2 Rewrite the sentence below correctly. There are four mistakes.

   mario wrote a letter to his cousin in san francisco

   _____

3 Mario wrote a letter to his cousin. He put the letter in an envelope. He wrote the address on the envelope. He put a stamp on the envelope. What will Mario do next?

   a. take the letter to school

   b. put the envelope in the mailbox

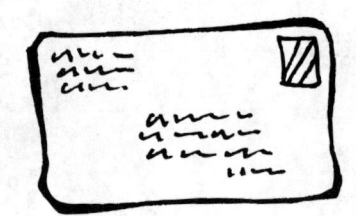

4 Circle the homophones in the sentence below.

   Some mail carriers are male.

5 Why do people write friendly letters?

   _____

   _____

Name _____ Date _____

Write to Persuade

1. I agree with Remy. We both think pink lemonade tastes great. What does it mean to agree?

    a. to think the same.   **b.** to think differently

---

2. I agree that ice cream is the best dessert.

    Is the word *agree* a noun or a verb? _____

---

3. To **persuade** means to make someone agree with you. Tom does not like soccer. You might persuade him to play anyway. Circle the choice below that shows a boy that you would have to persuade to play soccer.

    a.   **b.**

---

4. Circle the antonym for *agree*.

    a. fight   **b.** disagree

---

5. What might you try to persuade your parents to do?

_____

_____

_____

_____

Name _____ Date _____

Context Clues

1 **Context clues** help us understand the meaning of an unfamiliar word. Context clues are usually found in the words surrounding an unknown word. Use context clues in the sentence below to find the answer.

Sharon overslept and missed the bus. Sharon was _____ for school.

a. early

b. late

2 Write the correct word choice in the sentence below.

I understand the three _____ Mrs. Green read.

paragraph   paragraphs   paragraphes

3 Kevin plays at recess. He kicks the ball hard. He kicks it into the net. What is Kevin playing?

_____

4 Find a word in Sentence A that is a homophone of a word in Sentence B. Circle the two homophones.

A. Can you guess which gift I sent?

B. It cost me three dollars and one cent.

5 Think of a classmate. Write three clues that would help someone guess who you are thinking about.

_____   _____   _____

48

Name _____ Date _____

Summaries

1 A **summary** is a short explanation that tells what happens in a story. It includes the important events. Circle the choice below that gives a summary.

    a. Cinderella went to a ball and met the Prince. Cinderella lost her slipper. The Prince returned it.

    b. Cinderella has a fairy godmother. Her step-mother is mean. The slipper was pretty.

2 Write the correct word choice in the sentence below.

    The word *summary* is a _____.
                                          noun   verb

3 If you tell a summary after you read a story, you will _____ the story better.

    a. forget   **b.** remember

4 Complete the sentence below by writing an antonym for *beginning*.

    A helpful summary tells what happens at the beginning, middle, and _____ of a story.

5 Circle the word in the sentence below that has a prefix.

    A summary leaves out unimportant details.

Name _____ Date _____

Following Directions

1 We must follow directions to learn in school. We can read directions. We can hear directions. How would you follow directions in physical education class?

    a. by reading   **b.** by hearing

2 Identify the type of sentence below.

Do your homework now.

    a. statement   **c.** command

    b. question   **d.** exclamation

3 Read all of the directions carefully. Then do only what is asked.

    A. Write your name. _____
    B. Stand up.
    C. Sit down.
    D. Clap your hands three times.
    E. Follow only Direction A.

4 My mother will ground me for not following directions. The word *ground* means:

    a. to stop a plane from flying   **b.** to make somebody stay home

5 What is one direction you follow at school every day?

_____

Name _____   Date _____

Cause and Effect

1. A **cause** tells why something happens. An **effect** tells the result of what happened. Circle the words in the sentence below that tell the cause.

We had a lot of rain, so I took an umbrella.

....

2. Write the plural form of each of the following nouns.

a. dog _____   c. study _____

b. tree _____   d. apple _____

....

3. I went to the park with my family on Saturday. It was a very sunny day. The sun was shining so brightly that I had to wear my sunglasses all day. Circle the choice that tells the effect in this story.

a. I went to the park

b. I had to wear my sunglasses

....

4. Find a word in Sentence A that is a homophone of a word in Sentence B. Circle the two words.

A. It was cold, so I wore a coat.   B. Mom likes to sew.

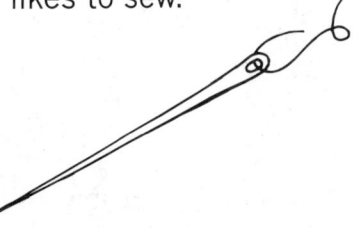

....

5. Complete the sentence below with an effect.

It was a hot day, so I _____

_____

51

Name _____ Date _____

Fact or Opinion

1 A **fact** is a true statement. It can be proven. Circle the choice below that states a fact.

  a. Puppies wag their tails.

  b. A dog is the best pet.

2 Identify the type of sentence below.

  A frog has a long, sticky tongue.

  a. statement

  b. question

  c. command

  d. exclamation

3 An **opinion** is a statement that tells what someone thinks. It is *not* a fact. Luis and Edgar were talking about fish. Luis said, "Fish have gills and fins." Edgar said, "Fish are fun pets." Who gave an opinion?

  a. Luis   **b.** Edgar

4 Choose the synonym for the word *opinion*.

  a. opposite   **b.** belief

5 Finish the sentence below with your opinion.

  I think that cats are _____

  _____

52

Language Boosters • Gr. 3 © 2009 Creative Teaching Press

Name _____   Date _____

Telling Time

1 Some clocks are **digital.** Digital clocks show time using numbers, such as 3:26. Some clocks are **analog.** Analog clocks show time using hands that point to numbers in a circle. Write the correct name of each clock on the line below it.

a.   b.

_____   _____

2 **To form the plural for most words ending in -s, -x, -sh, or -ch,** you must add *-es* to the end of the word. For example: dress–dress**es**; church–church**es.** Write the plural form for each of the following nouns.

a. clock _____   c. watch _____

b. finish _____   d. minute _____

3 Before Alex can go to the party, she has to finish her homework and wrap the present. Alex looked at her watch. It said 5:50. The party starts at 6:00. Alex will probably be:

a. late   b. on time

4 Draw a line from each sentence to the correct picture.

1. The coach used a stopwatch to time the runner.   a.

2. My mom checked her watch for the correct time.   b.

5 When do you use a watch? _____

Name _____ Date _____

Money

1. We use money to buy, or purchase, items. Circle the choice that shows a person purchasing milk.

a.   b.

---

2. Circle the three nouns in the sentence below.

Alan spends money on books.

---

3. Miranda went shopping. She had $50.00. She bought clothes. The clothes cost $40.00. Did Miranda have enough money?

_____

---

4. Find a word in Sentence A that is a homophone of a word in Sentence B. Circle the two words.

A. Be careful when spending money.

B. The bee flew around the flower.

---

5. How do you like to spend your money?

_____

Name _____ Date _____

Addition

1. The answer to an addition problem is the **sum**. Circle the sum in the addition problems below.

a. 17 + 9 = 26
b. 20
   + 15

   35
c. 22 = 15 + 7

2. Circle the adverb in the sentence below.

Madison easily solved the two-digit addtion problem.

3. The **addends** are the numbers added together in an addition problem. Grace's sticker collection had 46 stickers. Grace received 15 more stickers for her birthday. Circle the choice that correctly shows the addends.

a. 15 + 61

b. 61 + 46

c. 46 + 15

4. Find a word in Sentence A that is a homophone of a word in Sentence B. Underline the two words.

A. Seventeen is the sum of eight plus nine.   **B.** Some problems are easier than others.

5. Circle the word below that is *not* used in addition.

add   plus   minus   sum

55

Name _____   Date _____

Subtraction

1 The answer to a subtraction problem is the **difference**. Circle the difference in the subtraction problems below.

  a. 20 – 13 = 7

  b. $\begin{array}{r} 36 \\ -12 \\ \hline 24 \end{array}$

  c. 12 = 18 – 6

---

2 Write the correct word choice in the sentence below.

  To subtract _____ to take away.

              mean   means

---

3 The **subtrahend** is the number subtracted in a subtraction problem. Jack had 30 marbles in a jar. His brother took 14 out of the jar. Jack has 16 marbles left. Circle the choice that shows the subtrahend.

  a. 16

  b. 30

  c. 14

---

4 Find a word in Sentence A that is an antonym of a word in Sentence B. Circle the two words.

  A. Sixteen minus nine equals seven.

  B. Sixteen plus nine equals twenty-five.

---

5 Circle the word below that is *not* used in subtraction.

  minus   take   away   sum   difference

Name _____   Date _____

Multiplication

1. The answer to a multiplication problem is the **product**. Circle the product in the multiplication problems below.

a. 8 x 9 = 72

b.
```
   7
 x 6
 ---
  42
```

c. 56 = 8 x 7

---

2. Write the correct word choice in the sentence below.

The word *multiply* is usually a _____.
                                      noun   verb

---

3. Multiplication is the same as repeated addition. Circle the choice that does *not* belong.

a. 8 + 8 + 8 + 8 = 32

b. 8 x 4 = 32

c. 32 – 8 = 24

---

4. Draw a line from each sentence to the correct picture.

1. I am learning the multiplication tables.

a.

8s		
8 x 0 = 0	8 x 4 = 32	8 x 8 = 64
8 x 1 = 8	8 x 5 = 40	8 x 9 = 72
8 x 2 = 16	8 x 6 = 48	8 x 10 = 80
8 x 3 = 24	8 x 7 = 56	

2. The tables are in the cafeteria.

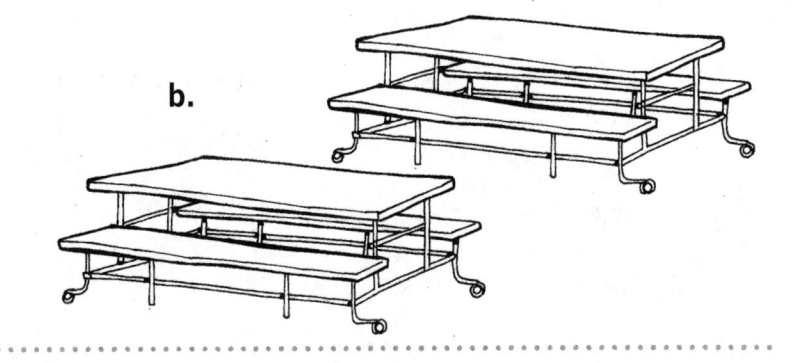

b.

---

5. Circle the choice below that describes multiplication.

a. nine plus seven

b. nine times seven

c. nine minus seven

Name _____ Date _____

Division

1 The answer to a division problem is a **quotient**. Circle the quotient in the division problems below.

a. 16 ÷ 2 = 8   b. 9)$\overline{63}$ with 7 above   c. 7 = 42 ÷ 6

---

2 Rewrite the sentence below correctly. There are four mistakes.

do we multiply or devid to find the correkt answer

_____

---

3 Division is the same as repeated subtraction. Circle the choice that does *not* belong.

a. 32 – 8 = 24; 24 – 8 = 16; 16 – 8 = 8; 8 – 8 = 0

b. 8 × 4 = 32

c. 32 ÷ 8 = 4

---

4 Circle the homophones in the sentence below.

We divided the eight cookies between us and ate them quickly.

---

5 Draw a line to match each math operation to its correct symbol.

addition   a. –

subtraction   b. ÷

multiplication   c. +

division   d. ×

Name _____ Date _____

Greater, Less, or Equal

1. Always start with the larger, or greater, number when subtracting. Circle the correctly written subtraction problem below.

   a. 17 − 9 = 8   **b.** 9 − 17 = 8

---

2. Identify the type of sentence below.

   Twelve plus eight is equal to eight plus twelve.

   $$12 + 8 = 8 + 12$$

   a. statement   **b.** question   **c.** command   **d.** exclamation

---

3. Joe has less money than Bobby. Bobby has more money than Luke. Luke has more money than Joe. Who has the most money?

   _____

---

4. Mrs. Beyer will add to find the greater number. In this sentence, the word *add* means:

   a. to put in an ingredient   **b.** to count up

---

5. Write the correct word choice in the sentence below.

   Fifty-three is _____ 53.

   greater than   less than   equal to

59

Name _____ Date _____

Estimation

1. To **estimate** means to guess an amount. It is not an exact number. Circle the choice that tells an estimate.

   a. The cat weighs about eight pounds.

   b. The cat weighs exactly eight pounds.

2. Write the correct word choice in the sentence below.

   Lisa poured nearly 20 _____ into the jar.
                                    candy   candies

3. Joanie does her homework every night. It usually takes about 20 minutes. Is this an estimate or an exact number?

   _____

4. Find a word in Sentence A that is an antonym of a word in Sentence B. Circle the two words.

   A. Rick jumps about three feet.

   B. Rick jumps exactly three feet.

5. When do you use estimation?

   _____

60

Name _____ Date _____

Place Value

1 **Place value** is the value of a digit in a number. Circle the choice that tells the place value.

a. 3 + 2 = 5

b. three tens and two ones = 32

2 Write the plural form for each of the following nouns.

> 6,497

a. one _____

b. ten _____

c. hundred _____

d. thousand _____

3 There are 10 ones in one ten. There are 10 tens in one hundred. There are _____ hundreds in one thousand.

a. 10

b. 20

c. 30

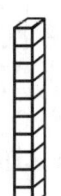

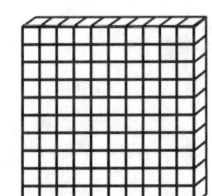

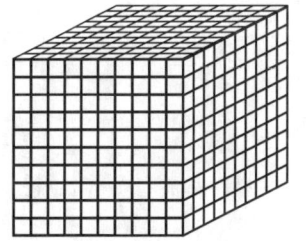

4 Write the correct word choice in the sentence below.

Please study your math _____ now.
                            fax   facts

5 The baseball card is easy to get. It is a dime a dozen. The idiom *a dime a dozen* means:

a. common

b. not common

Name _____   Date _____

Fractions

1. A **fraction** is a part of a whole thing or group of things. Circle the choice that shows a rectangle that is broken into fractions.

a.

1

b.

$\frac{1}{4}$	$\frac{1}{4}$
$\frac{1}{4}$	$\frac{1}{4}$

2. Circle the two nouns in the sentence below.

Our teacher makes fractions easy to understand.

3. Jennifer measured half a cup of milk. Circle the choice that shows half a cup of milk.

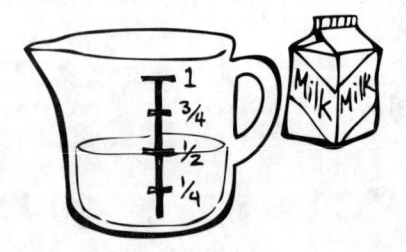

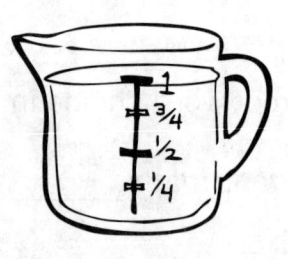

a.   b.

4. Circle the antonym of the word *fraction*.

a. whole   b. part of a whole

5. That's not fair! It's only a fraction of what I deserve. In this sentence *only a fraction of* means:

a. more than   b. less than   c. equal to

Name _____ Date _____

Decimals

1 A **decimal** shows parts of a whole number. The first two numbers after the decimal point show tenths and hundredths. Circle the choice that shows a decimal.

   a. 0.3

   b. 3/10

   c. 3

2 Write the correct word choice in the sentence below.

   Money amounts are _____ with a decimal point.

   writed   written

3 There are 100 cents in a dollar. If something costs 99 cents, it costs 99 _____ of a dollar.

   a. tenths   b. hundredths

4 Find a word in Sentence A that is an antonym of a word in Sentence B. Circle the two words.

   A. Lena bought one whole pie.

   B. Lena bought one part of another pie.

5 Write five-tenths as a decimal.

   _____

Name   Date

Temperature

1. **Temperature** is the degree of heat or cold. The hotter something is, the greater its temperature is. The cooler something is, the lower its temperature is. Circle the choice that shows the greater temperature.

a.   b.

2. Identify the type of sentence below.

The snowstorm dropped 10 inches of snow on the ground.

a. question   **b.** exclamation   **c.** statement   **d.** command

3. The meteorologist said the temperature will be 100 degrees outside today. "That's awfully hot!" exclaimed Andrew. What should Andrew wear on a day like today?

_____

4. Read the sentences below. Then circle the two synonyms for the word *freezing*.

The temperature was freezing. It was 20 degrees below zero.

a. warm   **b.** frigid   **c.** cold   **d.** tepid

5. Write about a time when the temperature was uncomfortable.

_____

_____

_____

64

Name _____   Date _____

Length

1 **Length** is a measurement of how long something is from end to end. Circle the choice that shows a measure of length.

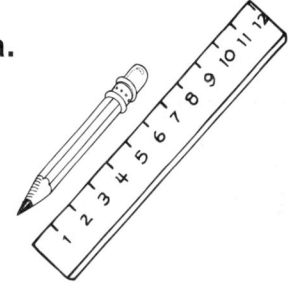

a.   b.

2 Rewrite the sentence below correctly. There are four mistakes.

how long is chelseys hair

_____

3 We use inches or centimeters to measure small items. We use meters or yards to measure large items. Circle the choice below that you would measure by using inches or centimeters.

a.   b.

4 Find a word in Sentence A that is a synonym of a word in Sentence B. Circle the two words.

A. It is a short walk to the library.

B. It is a brief walk to the park.

5 I would use a yardstick to measure the length of _____

_____

65

Name   Date

Capacity

1. **Capacity** is the amount of three-dimensional space that something can hold. Circle the choice that shows a measure of capacity.

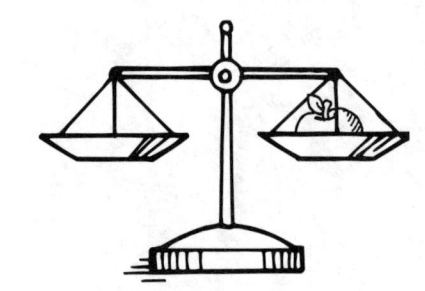

a.   b.

---

2. Write the correct word choice in the sentence below.

There are four _____ in a gallon.
           quart   quarts

---

3. A measuring cup has a smaller capacity of water than a swimming pool. What has a larger capacity of water than a swimming pool?

_____

---

4. **Homographs** are words that are spelled the same (and sometimes sound the same) but have different meanings. Find a word in Sentence A that is a homograph of a word in Sentence B. Circle the two words.

A. The capacity of a can of soda is 12 ounces.

B. I can pour myself a glass of juice.

---

5. Think about objects you see in the grocery store. Name one object in the grocery store that has capacity.

_____

Name _____ Date _____

Weight

1. The heaviness of an object is its **weight**.
What is your weight?

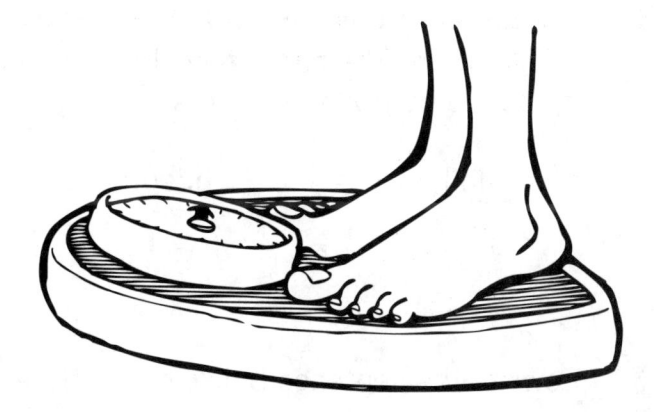

_____

2. Rewrite the sentence below correctly. There are three mistakes.

the weight of the elefant is 1,000 kilograms

_____

_____

3. A blue whale is the largest animal on earth. An adult blue whale's _____ is 418,000 pounds.

a. weight

b. volume

4. Circle the antonym of the word *heavy*.

a. strong			b. light

5. Write the correct word choice in the sentence below.

The baby _____ almost seven pounds.
                weigh   weighing   weighs

67

Name _____ Date _____

Graphs

1. A **graph** helps us compare numbers and information. The bar graph shown makes it easy to compare amounts of:

  a. rainfall   b. summer

Rainfall Spring 2007

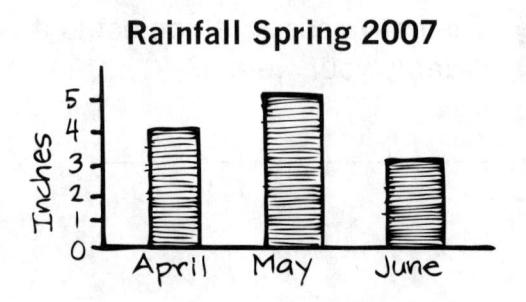

2. Rewrite the sentence below correctly. There are four mistakes.

i mad a lin graph to show rainfall amounts

_____

3. A **pictograph** uses pictures to compare information. Circle the pictograph choice.

a.

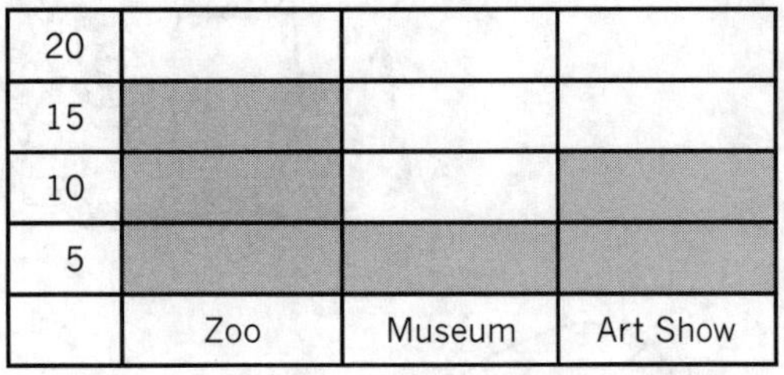

20			
15			
10			
5			
	Zoo	Museum	Art Show

b.

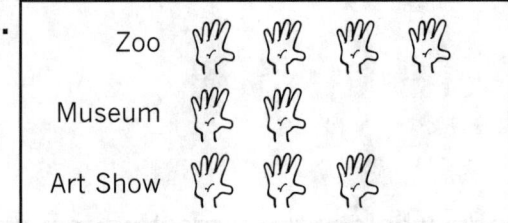

| Zoo |
| Museum |
| Art Show |

4. Find a word in Sentence A that is an antonym of a word in Sentence B. Circle the two words.

A. The information is a little disorganized.

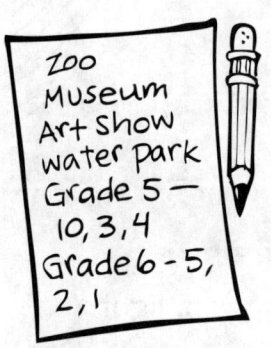

Zoo
Museum
Art show
water park
Grade 5 —
10, 3, 4
Grade 6 — 5, 2, 1

B. A graph helps us show information in an organized way.

	Zoo	Museum	Art Show
grade 5	10	3	4
grade 6	5	2	1

5. The graph in question number 4 shows _____.

Name _____ Date _____

Geometry

1 **Geometry** is the study of shapes and solid figures. A **shape** is a flat form that has height and length. A **solid figure** is a 3-dimensional form that has height, length, and depth. Circle the choice below that shows a solid figure.

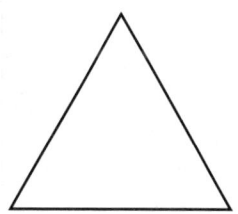

a. b.

2 Circle the two adjectives in the sentence below.

The round ball bounced on the basketball court.

3 An octagon is a shape that has eight sides. It looks like a stop sign. Circle the choice that shows an octagon.

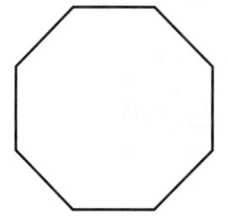

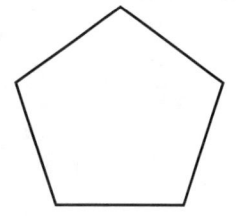

a. b.

4 Find a word in Sentence A that is a homophone of a word in Sentence B. Circle the two words.

A. A flower looks the same on all sides.

B. Don't put too much flour in the cake.

5 Lisa and Suzanna are like two peas in a pod. They both do well in geometry, spelling, and sports. *Two peas in a pod* means that Lisa and Suzanna:

a. are not very much alike

b. are very much alike

69

Name _____ Date _____

Area

1 Area is the surface measurement of a shape or a solid figure. Area is measured in square units. If you count up the square units of a figure, you will know its area. What is the area of the rectangle below?

   a. 10 square units

   b. 20 square units

   c. 30 square units

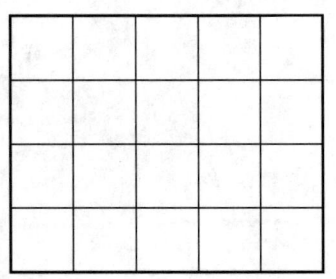

2 Rewrite the sentence below correctly. There are four mistakes.

the equation for aera looks like this: length × width = aera

_____

3 Area is measured in square units. For which figure would it be easier to find the area?

   a.   **b.**

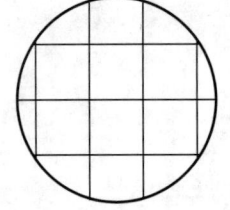

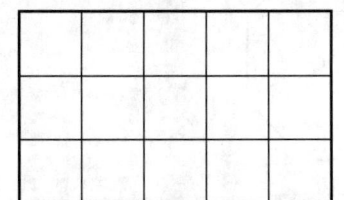

4 Find a word in Sentence A that is a homophone of a word in Sentence B. Circle the two words.

   A. Tom finished the whole page on area.

   B. There is a hole in the bucket.

5 Which of the following objects could you use to figure out the area of your desk?

   a.   **b.**

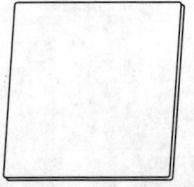

Name _____   Date _____

Perimeter

1. The **perimeter** of a figure is the length around the entire closed figure. Length shows the measurement of one side. Perimeter shows the length of all sides combined. Circle the choice that shows perimeter.

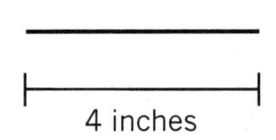

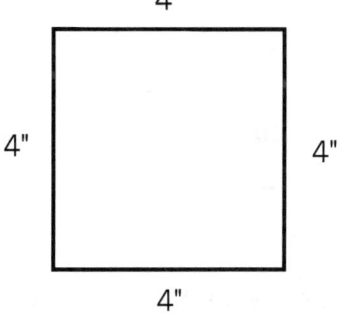

a. _____
   4 inches

b. [square with 4" on each side]

---

2. Identify the type of sentence below.

Will adding all sides of a figure give you its perimeter?

a. statement   **b.** question   **c.** command   **d.** exclamation

---

3. Measuring perimeter is really quite easy. You just need to remember to add the measurements on every side of the figure. What numbers would you add to find the perimeter of this rectangle?

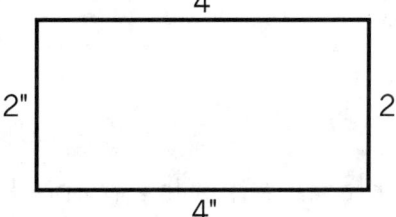

_____

[rectangle: 4" top, 4" bottom, 2" left, 2" right]

---

4. The plane figure was flat with four sides. In this sentence, the word *plane* means:

a. flat or level surface   □   **b.** airplane

---

5. Write the correct word choice in the sentence below.

Mrs. Casey asked us to _____ the perimeter of
                        measures   measuring   measure

our desktops.

71

Name _____ Date _____

Plane Figures

1. A **plane figure** is a flat shape. Circle the choice that shows a plane figure.

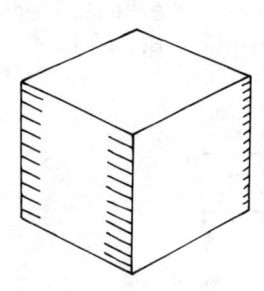

a.   b.

---

2. Rewrite the sentence below correctly. There are three mistakes.

what do you call a polygon with six sids

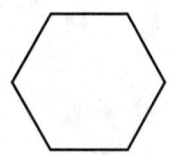

_____

---

3. A **polygon** is a plane figure. A polygon is made of three or more straight lines. Circle the choice that shows a polygon.

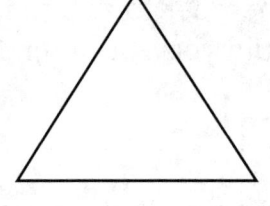

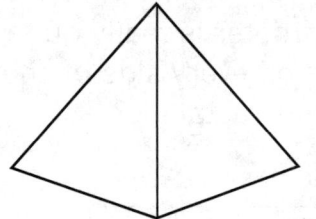

a.   b.

---

4. Find a word in Sentence A that is a homophone of a word in Sentence B. Circle the two words.

A. An octagon has eight sides.

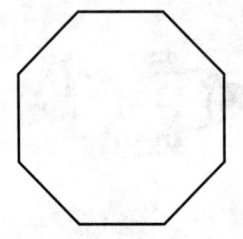

B. I ate a large slice of pizza.

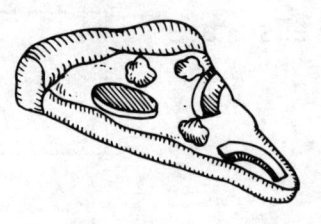

---

5. A triangle, a square, and a pentagon are all polygons. Name another type of polygon.

_____

Name _____   Date _____

Solid Figures

1. A **solid figure** is *not* flat. It has depth. Circle the choice that shows a solid figure.

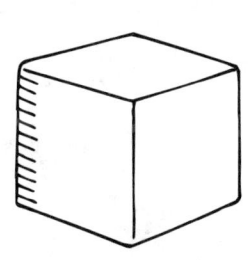

a.   b.

2. Rewrite the sentence below corretly. There are four mistakes.

a cube has twlve eges

_____

3. A **cylinder** has straight sides. The ends of a cylinder are curved. Circle the choice that shows a cylinder.

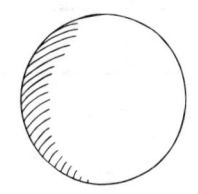

a.   b.

4. Circle the antonyms in the sentence below.

Raul put two large scoops of ice cream on one small cone.

5. Draw a solid figure and label it.

Name _____ Date _____

Angles

1 When two lines meet, they form an **angle.**
Circle the three angles in the triangle.

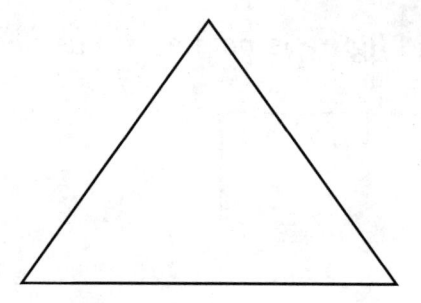

2 The two lines formed an angle. In this sentence, the word *angle* is a:

   a. noun   **b.** verb

3 Write the correct word choice in the sentence below.

   Parallel lines never touch. They _____ form an angle.
   always   never

   _____

4 Find a word in Sentence A that is an antonym of a word in Sentence B. Circle the two words.

   A. Parallel lines do not form angles.   **B.** Perpendicular lines form right angles.

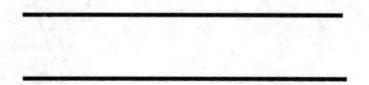

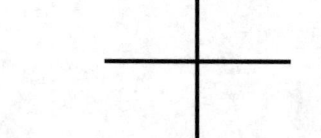

5 Draw a square.
Circle the angles formed by the square.
How many angles are formed?

_____

Name _____   Date _____

Problem-Solving Steps

1 You can use these five steps to help you solve a word problem: (1) read the problem; (2) circle the important numbers; (3) underline the question; (4) decide if you are going to add, subtract, multiply, or divide; and (5) solve the problem. The word *solve* means:

a. to find the answer **b.** to guess **c.** to read aloud

2 Circle the verb in the sentence below.

Michelle quickly solved each word problem.

3 Read the following word problem. Which step has *not* been completed? Look back at Problem 1 to help you.

a. Step 1

b. Step 3

c. Step 5

There were ⑥ fish bowls with ④ fish in each bowl. <u>How many fish are there in all?</u>

6 x 4 = ____

4 Shanna knew that the word problem was a five-step problem. In this sentence, the word *problem* means:

a. a question to be solved **b.** a difficult thing

5 Write the correct word choice in the sentence below.

If you get the problem wrong, you will have to _____ it.
did   redo   doing

Name _____ Date _____

Probability

1 **Probability** is a measure of how likely something is to happen. If there are three dotted marbles in a bag and one striped marble in that same bag, it is probable that I will pull out:

   a. a dotted marble

   b. a striped marble

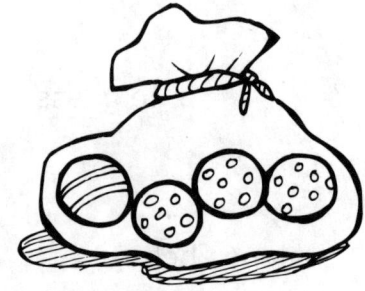

2 Write the correct word choice in the sentence below.

   Ralph pulled three cards out of the deck. He probably

   _____ both red and black cards.
      has   have

3 The weather reporter said there is a small chance for rain. Circle the choice that is a true statement.

   a. It might rain.　　　　**b.** It will rain.

4 Find a word in Sentence A that is an antonym of a word in Sentence B. Circle the two words.

   A. It is likely that you will roll a six once in six throws.

   B. It is unlikely that you will roll a six twice in two throws.

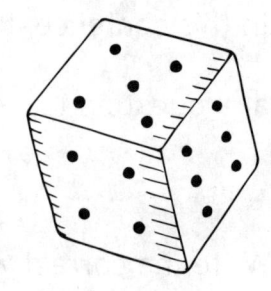

5 The gum ball machine has more green gum balls than red gum balls. What do you think is likely to happen?

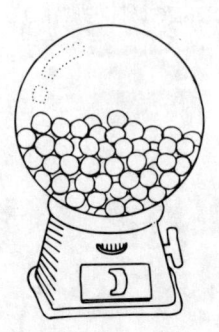

   _____

   _____

Name _____ Date _____

Inverse Operations

1 Addition and subtraction are **inverse operations**. Multiplication is the inverse operation of:

a. subtraction

b. addition

c. division

$9 + 6 = 15 \quad 15 - 9 = 6 \quad 5 \times 6 = 30 \quad 30 \div 5 = 6$

---

2 Identify this type of sentence: Do the inverse operation for that math problem.

a. statement   b. question   c. command   d. exclamation

---

3 Carmen needed to do the inverse operation for this math problem: $9 \times 5 = 45$. Carmen wrote $9 + 5 = 14$. Was Carmen correct? Explain.

_____

_____

---

4 Circle the antonym of the word *problem*.

a. count   b. solution   c. total   d. subtraction

---

5 Learning inverse operations is so easy. I really understand them. It was a piece of cake! Circle the choice that shows the meaning of the idiom *a piece of cake*.

a. (boy reading book thinking "This is easy!")

b. (slice of cake on a plate)

77

Mammals

1. **Mammals** are animals that have hair or fur. Most female mammals give birth to live young. They feed their young with milk. Circle the choice that is a mammal.

    a. a tiger   **b.** a fish

2. Write the plural form of each of the following nouns that end in *-y*. Remember to change the *-y* to *-i* and then add *-es* to the end of the word to form its plural.

    a. baby   **b.** lady   **c.** puppy   **d.** pony

_____   _____   _____   _____

3. Write the correct word choice in the sentence below.

    A _____ is a mammal.
        snake   fox

4. Circle the antonym of the word *together*.

    Koalas are mammals that live alone.

5. Name three mammals.

_____   _____   _____

Name   Date

Fish

1. **Fish** lay eggs. A baby fish takes care of itself as soon as it hatches. What does the word *hatches* mean?

   a. comes out of an egg

   b. lives a long life

2. Circle the adjective in the sentence below.

   A fish has scaly skin.

3. Fish are cold-blooded, scaly animals that live in water. Fish breathe with their gills and swim with their fins. They differ in size, from as small as half an inch to as long as 65 feet! Which choice below is true about fish?

   a. Fins help fish to breathe.

   b. Fish come in lots of different sizes.

4. Find a word in Sentence A that is a homophone of a word in Sentence B. Circle the two words.

   A. A fish uses its tail to swim.

   B. My dad told a funny tale about fishing.

5. I forgot my homework. It was the first time. My teacher smiled and said, "You are off the hook this time! Next time you will have to stay in at recess." What does *off the hook* mean?

   a. not in trouble

   b. in big trouble

Name _____   Date _____

Birds

1) **Birds** are animals with feathers and wings. They lay eggs, and most birds are able to fly. Birds are commonly found in marshes, woodlands, and forests, but they also live in deserts and polar regions. The word *commonly* means:

   a. never   **b.** always   **c.** usually

---

2) Write the plural form for each of the following nouns.

   a. pigeon _____   **c.** turkey _____

   b. finch _____   **d.** canary _____

---

3) Two birds fly in and out of a bush. They carry twigs in their beaks. They are probably:

   a. building a nest

   b. playing a game

---

4) Find a word in Sentence A that is an antonym of a word in Sentence B. Circle the two words.

   A. Some birds are too heavy to fly.

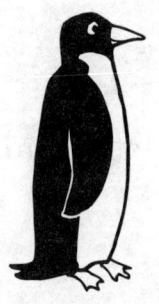

   B. Most birds are light enough to fly.

---

5) My favorite store is having a sale. I want to get there early because the early bird gets the worm! What does *the early bird gets the worm* mean?

   a. It's good to be early.

   b. It's good to be late.

80

Name _____   Date _____

Insects

1. **Insects** are small animals with six legs. Many insects have a pair of wings. Their bodies are divided into three parts. The word *divided* means:

   a. separated   **b.** joined   **c.** shared

2. Write the correct word choice in the sentence below.

   Insects _____ two antennae.
              have   has

3. Many insects have different stages in life. A caterpillar becomes a butterfly. This is called a **metamorphosis**. A *metamorphosis* is a _____.

   a. food

   b. change

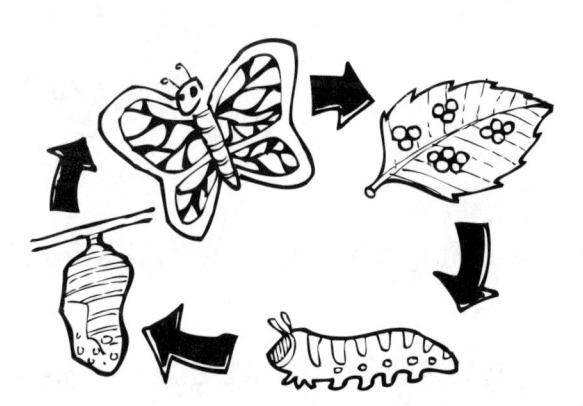

4. Find the words in Sentence A and Sentence B that are homographs (spelled the same but with different meanings). Circle the two words.

   A. The fly landed on the food.

   B. Most insects can fly.

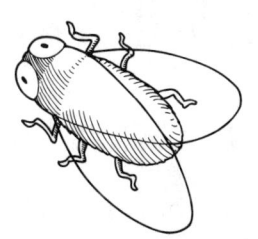

5. Name three insects.

_____   _____   _____

81

Name						Date

Spiders

1 **Spiders** are small animals that have eight legs and two poison fangs. Their bodies are divided into two parts. Spiders have many eyes and powerful jaws, which help them catch their prey. The word *powerful* means:

    a. strong   **b.** weak   **c.** huge

2 Circle the adjective in the sentence below.

Spiders spin sticky webs to catch prey.

3 A spider has fangs to bite its prey. The poison paralyzes the prey so it can't move. Poison is:

    a. something harmful

    b. something good

4 Find a word in Sentence A that is a homophone of a word in Sentence B. Circle the two words.

    A. A spider wraps its prey with silk.   **B.** Some people pray before a meal.

5 How do you feel about spiders?

_____

82

Name _____   Date _____

Vertebrates

1 A **vertebrate** is an animal that has a backbone. You have a backbone. A cat has a backbone. Circle the choice that shows an animal that has a backbone.

a.    b.    c.

2 Write the plural form of each of the following nouns.

a. amphibian    b. bird    c. mammal    d. reptile

_____   _____   _____   _____

3 A snake is a vertebrate. It has a flexible backbone that allows the snake to bend. The word *flexible* means:

a. bendable

b. stiff

4 Find a word in Sentence A that is a synonym of a word in Sentence B. Circle the two words.

A. All vertebrates have backbones.

B. Mammals, amphibians, birds, fish, and reptiles all have spines.

5 Add the prefix *in-* to the word *vertebrate* to complete the sentence.

An _____ does *not* have a spine.

83

Name _____   Date _____

Invertebrates

1 An **invertebrate** is an animal that does *not* have a spine. An ant does not have a spine. Circle the choice that shows another animal that does not have a spine.

a.   b.    c.

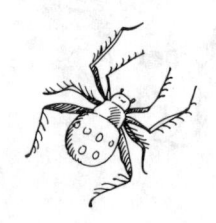

2 Write the correct word choice in the sentence below.

Invertebrates _____ no backbones.
                have   has

3 An insect is an invertebrate. Its body has three sections. A section is a:

a. part

b. whole

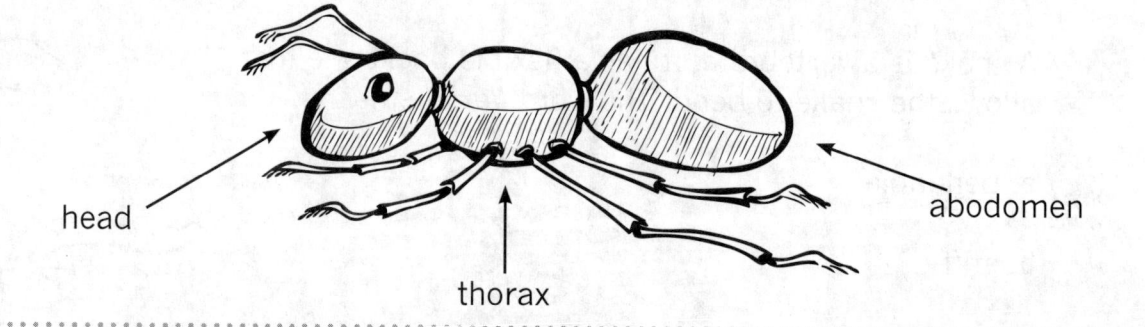

head   thorax   abodomen

4 Circle the antonyms in the sentence below.

Vertebrates and invertebrates are two very different types of animals.

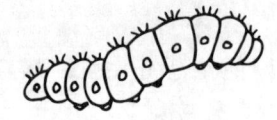

5 Circle the word in the sentence below that has a suffix.

An invertebrate is a spineless animal.

84

Name _____ Date _____

Body Systems

1 The **skeletal system** is made of bones. It gives your body shape and support. Circle the choice that shows a skeletal system.

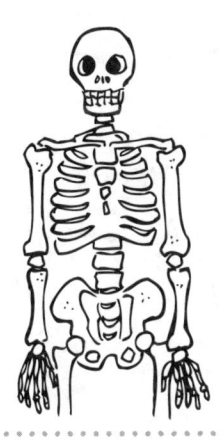

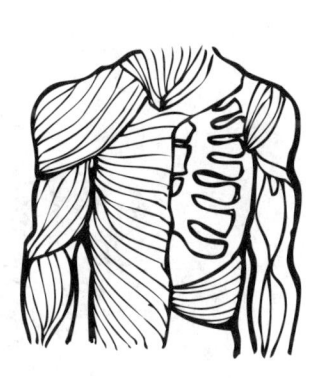

a. 　　　　　　　　　　　　　　　b.

2 Circle the verb in the sentence below.

The heart pumps blood through the body.

3 The **muscular system** is made of muscles. Muscles help us move our bodies. Circle the choice that shows a muscular system.

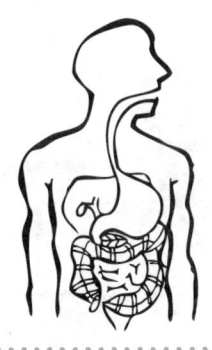

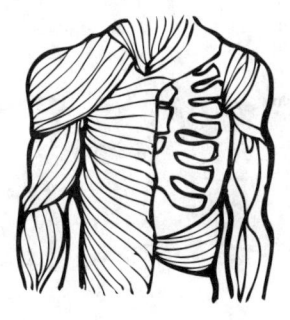

a. 　　　　　　　　　　　　　　　b.

4 Find a word in Sentence A that is a homograph of a word in Sentence B. Circle the two words.

A. An organ is a body part.

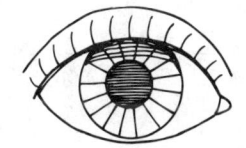

B. I can play the organ.

5 Write the correct word choice in the sentence below.

We would be _____ without muscles.
　　　　　　　　helpless　　helpful

Animal Defenses

1 Animals **defend** themselves in different ways. A turtle has a shell. The shell helps the turtle hide from danger. *Defend* means:

   a. to hurt

   b. to protect

2 Write the correct word choice in the sentence below.

   A porcupine _____ sharp quills.
                   has   have

3 Some animals have coats that help camouflage, or hide, them. A white rabbit can hide easily in:

   a. snow

   b. dirt

4 Complete the sentence below with the correct homophone.

   An animal that is not camouflaged is easy to _____.
                                           see   sea

5 Add the suffix *-ful* to the word *help* to complete the sentence below.

   It is _____ for animals to have ways of defending themselves.

Name _____ Date _____

Plant Adaptations

1 **Adaptations** are special features that help a plant survive in a special place. A cactus can survive in the desert because it stores water in its stems or leaves. The word *survive* means:

a. to live and grow

b. to die off

---

2 Circle the adjective in the sentence below.

Wildflowers grow in sunny fields.

---

3 Plants can live in water. Some of them have leaves that float so they get sunlight. Circle the choice that shows plants that float.

a.

b.

---

4 Find a word in Sentence A that is an antonym of a word in Sentence B. Circle the two words.

A. A plant can live when it gets sunlight.

B. A plant will die if it does not get sunlight.

---

5 Add the suffix *-ful* to the word *care* to complete the sentence below.

Be _____ not to give the plant too much water.

87

Name _____ Date _____

Ecosystems

1 An **ecosystem** is an environment. The desert is an ecosystem. The ecosystem includes the plants, animals, weather, and landforms of a place. Circle the choice that shows an ecosystem.

a.

b.

---

2 Write the plural form of each of the following nouns.

a. beach _____

b. bush _____

c. ranch _____

d. grass _____

---

3 Humans cut down many trees in the rain forest. Animals lose their homes and food. Doing this:

a. hurts the rain forest's ecosystem

b. helps the rain forest's ecosystem

4 Find a word in Sentence A that is a synonym of a word in Sentence B. Underline the two words.

A. Blue Water Lake has a stable ecosystem.

B. The ecosystem is steady.

---

5 Circle the word that has a prefix in the second sentence below.

A system is how something works. An ecosystem is how a part of the natural world works.

88

Name _____   Date _____

Natural Resources

1 **Natural resources** are things made by nature. Water is a natural resource. We use water for:

a. drinking

b. gas

2 Write the correct word choice in the sentence below.

Rocks and gems _____ natural resources we use for jewelry.
                  is   are

3 A **renewable resource** can be remade or regrown. Is a tree a renewable resource?

_____

4 We cannot drink polluted water. A synonym for *polluted* is:

a. dirty

b. clean

5 Circle the word that has a suffix in the sentence below.

We should not use earth's resources in a careless way.

89

Name _____   Date _____

Conservation

1 You can help conserve electricity. Turn off the light when you leave a room. What does the word *conserve* mean?

   a. to use

   b. to save

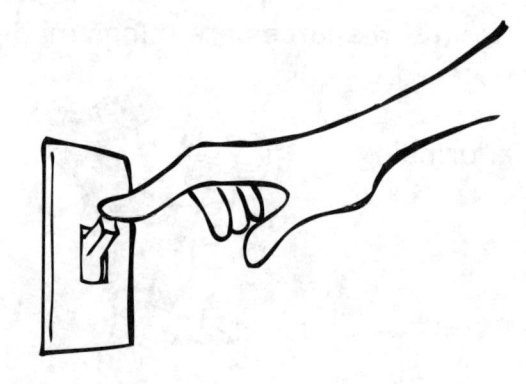

2 Circle the two verbs in the sentence below.

   Don't use lots of water to brush your teeth.

3 Recycle your soda cans. The metal can be used again. What does it mean to *recycle*?

   a. to throw away

   b. to use again

4 Find a word in Sentence A that is an antonym of a word in Sentence B. Circle the two words.

   A. Don't waste paper towels.

   B. Save your plastic bags.

5 Name three ways we can conserve resources.

   _____   _____   _____

Name _____ Date _____

Water Cycle

1) A cycle means that the same things happen over and over again. Clouds, rain, and oceans are all part of the **water cycle.** Circle the choice that shows the water cycle.

a.

b.

2) Circle the verb in the sentence below.

Water evaporates into the air.

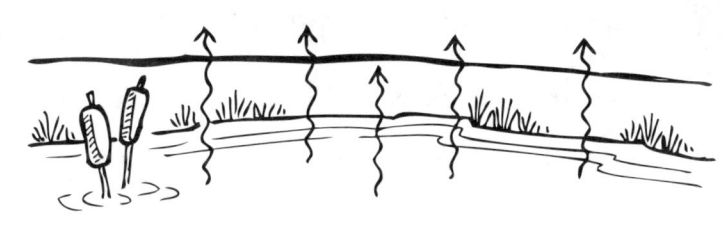

3) The water in the air rises and cools. It packs together to form condensation in the sky. Condensation makes:

a. clouds

b. clear skies

4) Circle the synonym of the word *rain*.

Take your umbrella. We will have precipitation today.

5) My dad was feeling under the weather. He needed to stay in bed. Circle the choice that shows what *under the weather* means.

a.

b.

Name _____   Date _____

Electricity

1 **Electricity** is energy. Electricity lights our homes and schools. Circle the choice that shows an object using electricity.

a.   b.

2 Circle the two verbs in the sentence below.

Ben Franklin proved that lightning is a form of electricity.

3 Thomas Edison improved the lightbulb. He invented one that would work for a long time. This means:

a. he made it worse

b. he made it better

4 Find a word in Sentence A that is an antonym of a word in Sentence B. Circle the two words.

A. The lightning was so bright it hurt my eyes.

B. The night was so dark I could not see anything.

5 Add the suffix -*ful* to the word *use* to complete the sentence below.

Electricity is very _____.

92

Name _____ Date _____

Solar System

1 Our **solar system** is made up of the planets and moons that orbit the sun. The sun is the center of the solar system. *Solar* means having to do with the:

   a. sun

   b. moon

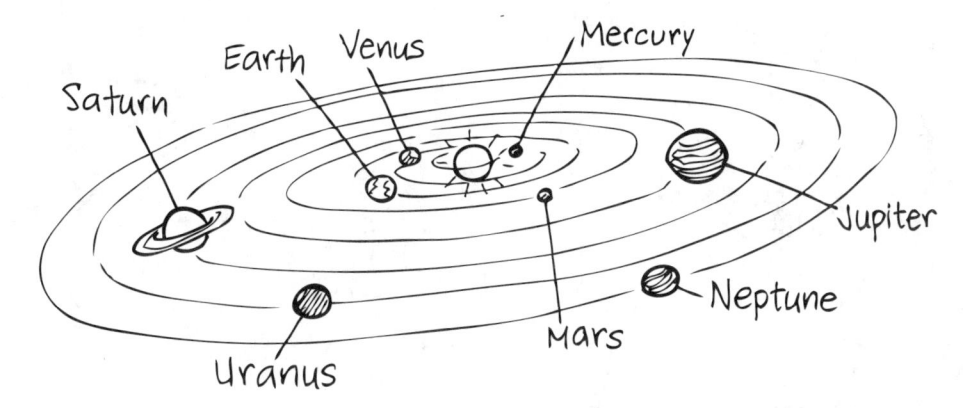

2 Which of the words below is a proper noun?

   a. planet   **b.** space   **c.** Saturn   **d.** solar system

---

3 The planets in our solar system orbit the sun. They move around it slowly. Orbit means:

   a. to move around   **b.** to stand still

---

4 Find a word in Sentence A that is a homophone of a word in Sentence B. Circle the two words.

   A. The sun is a huge star.   **B.** Mrs. Taylor has a son.

---

5 Circle the word that has a suffix in the sentence below.

   The sun's energy is powerful.

93

Name   Date

Geography

1. A **map** shows the location of countries, states, and cities. Circle the choice that shows a map.

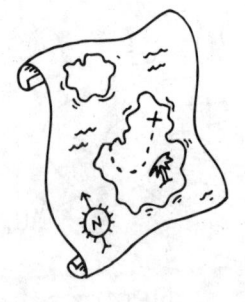

a.   b.

2. Circle the adjective in the sentence below.

Ivette saw a beautiful flower in Mexico.

3. "Let's go to Hawaii for vacation. I love going to islands," said Mom. "What's an island?" I asked. "That's easy," Mom replied. "An island is a piece of land that is surrounded by water. Let me draw an island for you." Circle the choice that shows Mom's picture.

a.   b.

4. Aunt Jessie lives far away from me. Circle two antonyms for the word *far*.

a. near   b. distant   c. close   d. alone

5. Write the correct word choice in the sentence below.

Learning to read a map can be _____.
                              challenge   challenged   challenging

Name _____   Date _____

Native Americans

1 **Native Americans** are indigenous people to North America. They may have been here longer than 20,000 years. The word *indigenous* means:

a. original

b. foreign

---

2 Write the correct word choice in the sentence below.

_____ Native Americans here before the pilgrims?
Was   Were

---

3 Native Americans taught Pilgrims how to plant corn. Native Americans taught Pilgrims how to fish. The Native Americans were:

a. helpful   b. unhelpful

---

4 Find a word in Sentence A that is a homograph of a word in Sentence B. Circle the two words.

A. The men hunted deer and other game for food.

B. Will you play a card game with me?

---

5 Write the correct word choice in the sentence below.

"Save the tomato seeds so we can _____ them next year," stated Dad.
plant   planted

95

Name _____ Date _____

Explorers

1 An **explorer** travels to new places. An explorer wants to find out more about these places. An explorer is someone who:

   a. searches for new things   **b.** works inside all day

---

2 Circle the three proper nouns in the sentence below.

De Leon found Florida and Puerto Rico.

---

3 Richard Byrd explored Antarctica. It is frigid in Antarctica. Richard Byrd probably wore _____ in Antarctica.

   a. a bathing suit

   b. a winter coat

---

4 Christopher Columbus is another famous explorer. Circle the synonym for the word *explorer.*

   a. traveler   **b.** renter   **c.** camper

---

5 Tell about a time that you went exploring.

_____

_____

_____

Name _____ Date _____

National Landmarks

1 A **national landmark** is a building or an area that has been preserved because it is important to our country. Circle the choice that shows a national landmark.

a.

b.

2 Write the correct word choice in the sentence below.

There _____ many national landmarks in the United States.
        is   are

3 The president of the United States lives in the White House. The building of the White House started in 1792. It was completed in 1800. The White House is a national landmark. _____ lived in the White House.

a. Abraham Lincoln   **b.** Christopher Columbus

4 Find a word in Sentence A that is a homophone of a word in Sentence B. Circle the two words.

A. I will see you at the Grand Canyon this summer.

B. She sailed across the sea last year.

5 Write the correct word choice in the sentence below.

It is important to _____ national landmarks.
              visiting   visit   visitor

Name   Date

Our Government

1 The **Constitution** of the United States of America is the supreme source of all government powers in the United States. The word *supreme* means:

   a. most expensive   **b.** most important

2 Circle the adverb in the sentence below.

   The president spoke loudly at the conference.

3 We elect the leaders of our country. We do this by choosing who we think would do the best job. When we elect our leaders, we:

   a. vote   **b.** write them letters   **c.** call them on the phone

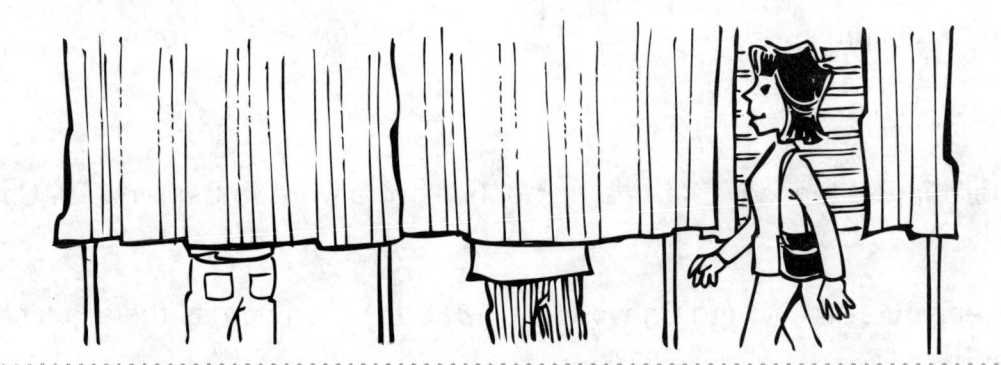

4 A governor is the head of a state. In this sentence, the word *head* means:

   a. skull   **b.** person in charge

5 In the mayor's speech, he said the key to success is to work hard and to get an education. The idiom *key to success* means:

   a. how to do well   **b.** how to fail

Name _____   Date _____

Rules and Laws

1 It is a **law** to wear a seatbelt. It is a **rule** to be kind to others. Laws must be obeyed. Rules are nice to obey. Is doing the dishes after dinner a rule or a law?

_____

2 Write each underlined word in its plural form.

a. Raise your <u>hand</u> before speaking.   _____

b. Put the <u>dictionary</u> on the shelf.   _____

c. Please tape the <u>box</u> shut.   _____

3 In many states, it is a law to wear a bike helmet if you are under age 18. Kari fell off her bike. She was not wearing a helmet. A police officer scolded her. The police officer probably scolded her because

_____

4 Find a word in Sentence A that is a homophone of a word in Sentence B. Circle the two words.

A. We do need to follow all laws.

B. The morning dew shone on the grass.

5 Write about a rule you need to follow.

_____

Anne Hutchinson

1 Anne Hutchinson was a Puritan woman who emigrated in 1634 from England to America, where she could share her beliefs. Another word for *emigrated* is:

    a. sang   **b.** moved   **c.** wrote

2 Write the plural form of each of the following nouns.

    a. colony _____   **c.** leader _____

    b. belief _____   **d.** speech _____

3 Anne Hutchinson believed in freedom of speech. She believed in freedom of religion. Anne Hutchinson believed in freedom of thought. You can guess that Anne Hutchinson was probably a very _____ person.

    a. shy

    b. active

4 Find a word in Sentence A that is a homophone of a word in Sentence B. Circle the two words.

    A. Anne carried a pail of water.   **B.** Anne's skin is quite pale.

5 Some people were angry with Anne Hutchinson. They did not agree with her beliefs. They had an axe to grind with her. The idiom *an axe to grind* means:

    a. to strongly disagree

    b. to strongly agree

Name _____ Date _____

Thomas Jefferson

1. The **Declaration of Independence** is a written document. It states that all people have the right to freedom and happiness. A document is:

   a. a record of information

   b. a play

---

2. Identify the type of sentence below.

Thomas Jefferson wrote the Declaration of Independence.

   a. statement   **b.** question   **c.** command   **d.** exclamation

---

3. Thomas Jefferson was the third president of the United States. Jefferson lived in Virginia. The name of his home was Monticello. When his presidency ended, he retired to Monticello. He died there in 1826. Thomas Jefferson:

   a. was president three times   **b.** lived in Monticello until his death

---

4. Thomas Jefferson was an excellent leader. Circle two synonyms for the word *leader*.

   a. head   **c.** follower

   b. chief   **d.** worker

---

5. Lisa had a field day when she visited Monticello. There were a lot of children there running all around. The idiom *had a field day* means:

   a. had lots of problems   **b.** had an enjoyable time

101

Name _____ Date _____

Frederick Douglass

1 Frederick Douglass was an African American who was born into slavery. He was forced to work as a slave for 20 years. Slaves are:

   a. not free people

   b. free people

2 Rewrite the sentence below correctly. There are four mistakes.

frederick douglass excaped from slavery

_____

3 Frederick Douglass was an abolitionist. He gave speeches. He wanted freedom for all African Americans. Douglass was _____ slavery.

   a. for   **b.** against

4 Find a word in Sentence A that is a synonym of a word in Sentence B. Circle the two words.

   A. Frederick Douglass wanted to be freed from slavery.

   B. African Americans were released from slavery.

5 How do you think it felt to be a slave?

_____
_____
_____

Name _____ Date _____

Clara Barton

1. Clara Barton always wanted to be a nurse. Her first patient was her brother when he fell off a beam in the family barn. Circle the choice that shows a *nurse*.

a.

b.

2. Clara Barton tried to nurse people back to health. In this sentence, the word *nurse* is used as a:

a. verb

b. noun

3. Clara Barton started the American Red Cross. During war time, she traveled with soldiers to help bring them back to health. She comforted them, too. Clara Barton always thought of others before she thought of herself. What kind of person was Clara Barton?

a. a selfish person

b. a caring person

4. Find a word in Sentence A that is a homophone of a word in Sentence B. Circle the two words.

A. His weight broke the beam in the barn.

B. He didn't have to wait long for the nurse to help.

5. Would you like to be a nurse? Why or why not?

_____

103

Name _____   Date _____

Eleanor Roosevelt

1 Eleanor Roosevelt cared very much about people in need. She spent much of her life trying to help underprivileged people. Because of this, she got the nickname "First Lady to the World." The word *underprivileged* means:

a. famous and wealthy

b. poor and needy

2 Write the correct word choice in the sentence below.

Eleanor Roosevelt was _____ caring and loving First Lady.
                                    a   an

3 The wife of the president of the United States is called the *First Lady*. Eleanor Roosevelt was the First Lady from 1933–1945. She was married to Franklin D. Roosevelt. Franklin D. Roosevelt was the:

a. First Man

b. president of the United States

4 Working to help people in need is a difficult job.

Circle the synonym of the word *difficult*:

a. easy

b. hard

5 The prefix *pre-* means *before*. Vanessa can't wait to preview the new book about Eleanor Roosevelt. The word *preview* means:

a. to view after

b. to view before

Name _____ Date _____

Martin Luther King Jr.

1. Martin Luther King Jr. was a preacher. He believed in Civil Rights. He wanted all people to be treated fairly. He wanted all people to be treated equally. Civil Rights are:

   a. rights we all have as human beings   **b.** rights only a few people have

2. Write the correct word choice in the sentence below.

   Reverend King's *I Have a Dream* speech _____ delivered on Augugst 28, 1965.

   (was   is)

3. In 1964 Martin Luther King Jr. received the Nobel Peace Prize for his work to help the Civil Rights Movement. You can guess that Reverend King is an _____ person in American history.

   a. unimportant   **b.** important

4. Find a word in Sentence A that is a homophone of a word in Sentence B. Circle the two words.

   A. Martin Luther King Jr. made many speeches.

   B. The maid cleaned the house.

5. Circle the compound word in the sentence below.

   Martin Luther King Jr. preached often during his lifetime.

Name _____   Date _____

Neil Armstrong

1. Neil Armstrong is a former astronaut. He was the first man to walk on the moon. An astronaut:

   a. travels to space

   b. drives fast cars

2. Write the correct word choice in the sentence below.

   The *Apollo 11* moon landing _____ place on July 20, 1969.

   took   takes

3. Neil Armstrong took his first plane ride at the age of six. He was fascinated with aviation ever since. You can probably guess that Neil Armstrong was interested in:

   a. flight

   b. boats

4. Circle the synonym for the word *curious*.

   Neil Armstrong was curious about flight.

   a. bored   **b.** interested   **c.** stupid

5. Would you like to walk on the moon? Why or why not?

   _____

Answer Key

Friends (Page 7)
1. a
2. happy
3. a
4. A. soft, B. prickly
5. b

Family (Page 8)
1. a
2. tall
3. b
4. A. aunt, B. ant
5. Answers will vary.

Pets (Page 9)
1. a
2. My pet turtle hid inside of his shell.
3. b
4. A. friends, B. enemies
5. rattlesnake, butterfly, blackbird

Hobbies (Page 10)
1. a
2. Tim's
3. a
4. A. likes, B. dislikes
5. Answers will vary.

Sports (Page 11)
1. Answers will vary.
2. fast
3. b
4. A. quicker, B. faster
5. c

Staying Fit (Page 12)
1. a
2. plays
3. a
4. A. wait, B. weight
5. c

Eating Healthy (Page 13)
1. a
2. grows
3. b
4. A. meet, B. meat
5. Answers will vary.

Feelings (Page 14)
1. a, b, e
2. lonely
3. b
4. A. mad, B. angry
5. Answers will vary.

Careers (Page 15)
1. a
2. tall
3. a
4. A. quiet, B. hushed
5. successful

My Community (Page 16)
1. b
2. is
3. a
4. A. eight, B. ate
5. Answers will vary.

At the Movies (Page 17)
1. b
2. quietly
3. a
4. 1—b, 2—a
5. Answers will vary.

At the Mall (Page 18)
1. b
2. purchased
3. b
4. a
5. sunglasses, salesclerk, supermarket, basketball

At the Bookstore (Page 19)
1. b
2. b
3. b
4. A. aloud, B. allowed
5. Answers will vary.

At a Restaurant (Page 20)
1. a
2. Emmanuel, fun, restaurant
3. 1—b, 2—a
4. A. real, B. reel
5. Answers will vary.

The Doctor's Office (Page 21)
1. a
2. Dr. Turner gave me medicine for my cough.
3. b
4. 1—a, 2—b
5. Answers will vary.

The Dentist's Office (Page 22)
1. b
2. shiny, white
3. b
4. A. exciting, B. boring
5. Answers will vary.

Holidays (Page 23)
1. a
2. We celebrate Valentine's Day in February.
3. b
4. A. normal, B. special
5. Answers will vary.

On Vacation (Page 24)
1. b
2. quickly
3. b
4. a
5. Answers will vary.

On the Road (Page 25)
1. b
2. tires, air
3. a
4. A. fast, B. speedy
5. a

On the Water (Page 26)
1. a
2. Ruby's
3. b
4. A. float, B. sinks
5. a

In the Air (Page 27)
1. a
2. hovered
3. a
4. A. plane, B. plain
5. b

107

Nouns (Page 28)
1. a, c, d
2. cup, juice
3. a, b
4. A. hair, B. hare
5. Answers will vary.

Verbs (Page 29)
1. a, b
2. d
3. a
4. A. smiles, B. frowns
5. Answers will very.

Adjectives (Page 30)
1. a—pretty, b—two, c—blue
2. The happy boy pet the little puppy.
3. bright, little, large
4. A. cold, B. cool
5. Answers will vary.

Adverbs (Page 31)
1. a—quickly, b—loudly, c—sadly
2. The shoemaker worked busily.
3. c
4. A. slowly, B. quickly
5. Answers will vary.

Sentences (Page 32)
1. a
2. c
3. a
4. read
5. Answers will vary.

Paragraphs (Page 33)
1. a
2. story, paragraphs
3. b
4. four
5. schoolhouse—b, bookcase—d, bookmark—a, textbook—c

Synonyms and Antonyms (Page 34)
1. a, c
2. a
3. b
4. A. likes, B. enjoys
5. Answers will vary.

Prefixes and Suffixes (Page 35)
1. unwraps
2. Ms. Thomas told us to reread the paragraph.
3. a
4. A. beginning, B. end
5. Answers will vary.

Idioms (Page 36)
1. a
2. Idioms can be difficult to learn.
3. b
4. A. blue, B. blew
5. a

Parts of a Book (Page 37)
1. a
2. pages
3. b
4. A. chapter, B. part
5. b

Authors (Page 38)
1. b
2. b
3. b
4. A. write, B. right
5. Answers will vary.

Illustrators (Page 39)
1. monkey
2. verb
3. illustrate
4. 1—a, 2—b
5. Answers will vary.

Fiction (Page 40)
1. b
2. d
3. a
4. read
5. Answers will vary.

Nonfiction (Page 41)
1. a
2. enjoys
3. b
4. write
5. Answers will vary.

Folktales (Page 42)
1. b
2. a—folktales, b—stories, c—biographies, d—authors
3. a
4. allowed, aloud
5. Answers will vary.

Biography and Autobiography (Page 43)
1. b
2. a
3. a
4. A. famous, B. well-known
5. a person's life

Write to Tell a Story (Page 44)
1. b
2. loves, write
3. c
4. A. hair, B. Hare
5. Answers will vary.

Write to Describe (Page 45)
1. b
2. sandwich
3. a
4. b
5. Answers will vary.

Write a Friendly Letter (Page 46)
1. a, c
2. Mario wrote a letter to his cousin in San Francisco.
3. b
4. mail, male
5. Answers will vary.

Write to Persuade (Page 47)
1. a
2. verb
3. a
4. b
5. Answers will vary.

Context Clues (Page 48)
1. b
2. paragraphs
3. soccer
4. A. sent, B. cent
5. Answers will vary.

Summaries (Page 49)
1. a
2. noun
3. b
4. end
5. unimportant

Following Directions (Page 50)
1. b
2. c
3. Child should only do Step A.
4. b
5. Answers will vary.

Cause and Effect (Page 51)
1. We had a lot of rain
2. a—dogs, b—trees, c—studies, d—apples
3. b
4. A. so, B. sew
5. Answers will vary.

Fact or Opinion (Page 52)
1. a
2. a
3. b
4. b
5. Answers will vary.

Telling Time (Page 53)
1. a—analog, b—digital
2. a—clocks, b—finishes, c—watches, d—minutes
3. a
4. 1—b, 2—a
5. Answers will vary.

Money (Page 54)
1. a
2. Alan, money, books
3. Yes
4. A. Be, B. bee
5. Answers will vary.

Addition (Page 55)
1. a—26, b—35, c—22
2. easily
3. c
4. A. sum, B. Some
5. minus

Subtraction (Page 56)
1. a—7, b—24, c—12
2. means
3. c
4. A. minus, B. plus
5. sum

Multiplication (Page 57)
1. a—72, b—42, c—56
2. verb
3. c
4. 1—a, 2—b
5. b

Division (Page 58)
1. a—8, b—7, c—7
2. Do we multiply or divide to find the correct answer?
3. b
4. eight, ate
5. addition—c, subtraction—a, multiplication—d, division—b

Greater, Less, or Equal (Page 59)
1. a
2. a
3. Bobby
4. b
5. equal to

Estimation (Page 60)
1. a
2. candies
3. estimate
4. A. about, B. exactly
5. Answers will vary.

Place Value (Page 61)
1. b
2. a—ones, b—tens, c—hundreds, d—thousands
3. a
4. facts
5. a

Fractions (Page 62)
1. b
2. teacher, fractions
3. a
4. a
5. b

Decimals (Page 63)
1. a
2. written
3. b
4. A. whole, B. part
5. 0.5

Temperature (Page 64)
1. a
2. c
3. Answers will vary.
4. b, c
5. Answers will vary.

Length (Page 65)
1. a
2. How long is Chelsey's hair?
3. a
4. A. short, B. brief
5. Answers will vary.

Capacity (Page 66)
1. a
2. quarts
3. Answers will vary.
4. A. can, B. can
5. Answers will vary.

Weight (Page 67)
1. Answers will vary.
2. The weight of the elephant is 1,000 kilograms.
3. a
4. b
5. weighs

Graphs (Page 68)
1. a
2. I made a line graph to show rainfall amounts.
3. b
4. A. disorganized, B. organized
5. students' test scores

Geometry (Page 69)
1. a
2. round, basketball
3. a
4. A. flower, B. flour
5. b

Area (Page 70)
1. b
2. The equation for <u>area</u> looks like this: length × width = <u>area.</u>
3. b
4. A. whole, B. hole
5. a

Perimeter (Page 71)
1. b
2. b
3. 2, 2, 4, 4
4. a
5. measure

Plane Figures (Page 72)
1. a
2. <u>Wh</u>at do you call a polygon with six sid<u>es</u>?
3. a
4. A. eight, B. ate
5. Answers will vary.

Solid Figures (Page 73)
1. b
2. <u>A</u> cube has tw<u>e</u>lve e<u>dges.</u>
3. a
4. large, small
5. Drawings will vary. Check for accuracy.

Angles (Page 74)
1. Check for accuracy.
2. a
3. never
4. A. Parallel, B. Perpendicular
5. 4

Problem-Solving Steps (Page 75)
1. a
2. solved
3. c
4. a
5. redo

Probability (Page 76)
1. a
2. has
3. a
4. A. likely, B. unlikely
5. I will get a green gum ball.

Inverse Operations (Page 77)
1. c
2. c
3. No. The inverse operation of multiplication is division.
4. b
5. a

Mammals (Page 78)
1. a
2. a—babies, b—ladies, c—puppies, d—ponies
3. fox
4. alone
5. Answers will vary.

Fish (Page 79)
1. a
2. scaly
3. b
4. A. tail, B. tale
5. a

Birds (Page 80)
1. c
2. a—pigeons, b—finches c—turkeys, d—canaries
3. a
4. A. heavy, B. light
5. a

Insects (Page 81)
1. a
2. have
3. b
4. A. fly, B. fly
5. Answers will vary.

Spiders (Page 82)
1. a
2. sticky
3. a
4. A. prey, B. pray
5. Answers will vary.

Vertebrates (Page 83)
1. c
2. a—amphibians, b—birds, c—mammals, d—reptiles
3. a
4. A. backbones, B. spines
5. invertebrate

Invertebrates (Page 84)
1. a
2. have
3. a
4. vertebrates, invertebrates
5. spineless

Body Systems (Page 85)
1. a
2. pumps
3. b
4. A. organ, B. organ
5. helpless

Animal Defenses (Page 86)
1. b
2. has
3. a
4. see
5. helpful

Plant Adaptations (Page 87)
1. a
2. sunny
3. b
4. A. live, B. die
5. careful

Ecosystems (Page 88)
1. b
2. a—beaches, b—bushes, c—ranches, d—grasses
3. a
4. A. stable, B. steady
5. ecosystem

Natural Resources (Page 89)
1. a
2. are
3. Yes, you can plant seeds or small trees to replace trees.
4. a
5. careless

Conservation (Page 90)
1. b
2. use, brush
3. b

4. A. waste, B. save
5. Answers will vary.

Water Cycle (Page 91)
1. b
2. evaporates
3. a
4. precipitation
5. a

Electricity (Page 92)
1. a
2. proved, is
3. b
4. A. bright, B. dark
5. useful

Solar System (Page 93)
1. a
2. c
3. a
4. A. sun, B. son
5. powerful

Geography (Page 94)
1. a
2. beautiful
3. b
4. a, c
5. challenging

Native Americans (Page 95)
1. a
2. Were
3. a
4. A. game, B. game
5. plant

Explorers (Page 96)
1. a
2. De Leon, Florida, Puerto Rico
3. b
4. a
5. Answers will vary.

National Landmarks (Page 97)
1. b
2. are
3. a
4. A. see, B. sea
5. visit

Our Government (Page 98)
1. b
2. loudly
3. a
4. b
5. a

Rules and Laws (Page 99)
1. a rule
2. a—hands, b—dictionaries, c—boxes
3. Answers will vary.
4. A. do, B. dew
5. Answers will vary.

Anne Hutchinson (Page 100)
1. b
2. a—colonies, b—beliefs, c—leaders, d—speeches
3. b
4. A. pail, B. pale
5. a

Thomas Jefferson (Page 101)
1. a
2. a
3. b
4. a, b
5. b

Frederick Douglass (Page 102)
1. a
2. Frederick Douglass escaped from slavery.
3. b
4. A. freed, B. released
5. Answers will vary.

Clara Barton (Page 103)
1. a
2. a
3. b
4. A. weight, B. wait
5. Answers will vary.

Eleanor Roosevelt (Page 104)
1. b
2. a
3. b
4. b
5. b

Martin Luther King Jr. (Page 105)
1. a
2. was
3. b
4. A. made, B. maid
5. lifetime

Neil Armstrong (Page 106)
1. a
2. took
3. a
4. b
5. Answers will vary.

English Language Development Proficiency Criteria

Strategies and Applications for Intermediate ELD Level

English Language Arts Substrand	K-2	3-5
Word Analysis: Decoding and Word Recognition	Recognize sound/symbol relationships and basic word-formation rules in phrases, simple sentences, or simple text. Recognize common abbreviations and simple prefixes and suffixes when attached to known vocabulary.	Recognize some common root words and affixes when attached to known vocabulary. Use knowledge of English morphemes, phonics, and syntax to decode and interpret the meaning of unfamiliar words in text.
Word Analysis: Concepts About Print	Recognize all uppercase and lowercase letters of the alphabet. Identify front and back cover and title page of a book. Follow words left to right and top to bottom on the printed page. Identify letters, words, and sentences by grade one.	
Vocabulary and Concept Development	Demonstrate internalization of English grammar, usage, and word choice by recognizing and correcting errors. Use decoding skills to read more complex words independently. Classify grade-appropriate categories of words. Use more complex vocabulary and sentences to communicate needs and express ideas in a wider variety of social and academic settings. Describe common objects and events in both general and specific language. Apply knowledge of content-related vocabulary to reading.	Demonstrate internalization of English grammar, usage, and word choice by recognizing and correcting errors. Use consistent standard English grammatical forms; however, some rules may not be followed. Use content-related vocabulary in reading.
Reading Comprehension	Ask and answer questions by using phrases or simple sentences.	Ask and answer questions by using phrases or simple sentences. Point out text features, such as title, table of contents, and chapter headings.
Writing: Organization and Focus	Produce independent writing that is understood but may include inconsistent use of standard grammatical forms. Write simple sentences appropriate for core content areas.	Produce independent writing that is understood but may include inconsistent use of standard grammatical forms. Begin to use a variety of genres in writing. Use more complex vocabulary and sentences appropriate for core content areas.
English-Language Conventions: Sentence Structure, Grammar, Punctuation, Capitalization, and Spelling	Produce independent writing that may include some inconsistent use of capitalization, periods, and correct spelling. Use standard word order but may have some inconsistent grammatical forms.	Produce independent writing that may include some inconsistent use of capitalization, periods, and correct spelling. Use standard word order but may have some inconsistent grammatical forms.

*Language proficiency criteria taken from the 2002 California ELD Standards